The Girl From Madison County

an extraordinary journey from the unexpected to a life
of purpose

Joan Sandergard

CDR Publishing

Published by CDR Publishing
Broken Arrow, Oklahoma 74012

Copyright © 2025 by Joan Sandergard

ISBN: 979-8-9921890-0-1

Manufactured in the United States of America

Cover and Book Design: Zealot Branding, Tulsa, Oklahoma

Photography: Michael McRuiz, Tulsa, Oklahoma

Content Warning

This memoir contains potentially disturbing content related to a broad spectrum of topics including sexual abuse, violence, child abuse, child neglect, self-harm, eating disorders, alcohol and drug abuse, suicide, and other sensitive material. It is deemed not appropriate for readers under twenty years of age. Please take into consideration your sensitivity and potential triggers when making an informed decision to read this book and take care of you.

Dedicated To

My daughter, Angel, the reason for the fights I fought. She kept me going when I wanted to give up, and she was the inspiration for my resilience and accomplishments. She is, and always will be, my everything.

To my mother, who never stopped believing in me, and is the reason I am here today.

To my father, forever my heart.

To my husband who left us too soon, you will always be in our hearts.

To my grandparents and uncle who were my rock and helped shape my life.

To my brother, my best friend.

For all my friends who believed in me when I couldn't believe in myself.

For my countless mentors who paved the way.

For all those who continue to fight for freedom from addiction, for social justice, and who stand in the gap. You are not alone.

To my younger self, who dared to fight against all odds, who fought endless battles alone, who never gave up and is the proof of the strength of the human spirit.

For my grandchildren, may you always remember the resiliency, strength, and overcoming in our family.

Acknowledgements

Thanks to Nikki Hanna, my writing coach, who championed me and helped me discover what I was born to do. Thanks to my editor, Robyn Conley, and reviewers Allen Elison, Joyce Hanewinkel, Cyma Shapiro, Mary Coley, and Beth Rengel. To my family and supporters who have encouraged and championed me: Jane Ooms, John Burrows, Mary Franck, Kay Meek, Jim Wallach, Cheryl Burrows, Jeanne Gambrell, Jeannette North, Vikki Bailey, Jeanean Doherty, Roberta Keenan, Carol Matza, Cindy Laughman Hughes, Jeroi Rott, Valerie Russell, Lorri Harper, Heather Buffington, Dawn Fox, Pam Waltz, Ty Hubbard, Rhonda Cunningham, Shahnaz Khalil, Nancy Ruth, Ree Kaplan, Liz Wicker, and Terry Kirkland. Their unwavering love and support kept me going during this life review. A big thanks to Heather Westover and Ana Maddox who gave me the fortitude and final push I needed to complete this book. I would like to express my gratitude to Carol Matza for her encouragement and contributions. A special thanks to Jeannette North and Beth Rengel who inspired me and believed in me. They are the reason this book happened. And to the numerous others whose love and support I couldn't have made it without.

If I can stop one heart from breaking,
I shall not live in vain;
If I can ease one life the aching,
Or cool one pain,
Or help one fainting robin
Unto his nest again,
I shall not live in vain.

Emily Dickinson

Contents

Preface

I sat cross-legged on the floor one day with pieces of a brand-new, seven-drawer desk spread around as I and a friend, who had graciously offered to help me assemble it, tried not to cry. We had spent three days struggling to assemble it while grappling with bewildering instructions and screws so tiny we could hardly hold them while screwing them in. Parts were put in backward or in the wrong places. Two drawers were jammed and something weird and unredeemable had happened in one of the corner connections. We entered this project thinking, "We are women, watch us roar," and ended up whipped, exhausted, devastated, and ready to count it all a loss.

My eyes were gritty, and my brain was foggy from studying microscopic instructions, trying to hold pieces together while holding a flashlight, and worrying about my older friend lying on her back in a crawl space with a hammer. Both she and the wonky desk were at risk.

Our failure gnawed at me. I wasn't ready to quit. Failure was never in my vocabulary. Instead of eating cherry pie, I called a friend down the street, who claimed to be "handy," and asked for her help. "Sure," she said. "I'll be right there." She waltzes in with an air of vitality and confidence and announces: "We are women, and we can do hard things." She grabbed a screwdriver and in short order redeemed the project.

Since then, I often thought of her words as I wrote this memoir. Although I found my stride in my thirties, the early years were challenging, and I knew recounting them would be hard. But I realized others could be helped by my story. It is one of hope, inspiration, purpose, and dedicating my life to helping others. Flush with messages for others about living a robust life and overcoming obstacles, it is a story about believing: *You can do hard things.*

Introduction

DISCOVERING WHAT YOU WERE BORN TO DO

As I wrote my story, I contemplated how my siblings and other family members would react to it. I realize that each child in a family has a unique experience growing up, and it is not unusual for siblings to ask, "Did we have the same parents?" My memories, no doubt, vary from those of my brother and sisters. Rebellious teenage years were unique to me, but there were reasons for my behavior at the time. The influences of those experiences on my early life were significant, and I would be remiss to leave them out.

My experiences and interpretations are my truth as I remember them. Memories are imperfect and at times my perspective may vary from those of others. Perceptions are subjective and uniquely shaped through a person's individual experiences, culture, background, and education. People are flawed. I candidly reveal my unfortunate missteps and explore the reasons for them.

I have been the object of injurious behavior, but it is not my intent to embarrass anyone other than myself or to cause hurt to others. I hold no malice toward anyone, and I hold myself accountable for my choices and behaviors. To protect others, I have changed names, tweaked minor facts, and endeavored to limit the focus to my perspective. Their stories are not mine to tell.

I reconciled with the players in those scenarios years ago. I write this story with the hope that my recovery will mean something to others who share similar experiences and that it will give them the courage to heal and overcome.

The approach to creating this memoir was to begin with a life review, to recount the events candidly, and to meet the challenge of being bold when writing about them. The result is a complicated and thorny story, ripe with raw emotions generated from a tsunami of events that left me knocked down, wounded, and fragile. It was *Bam! Bam! Bam!* I was free falling. But with a fire in my belly, I overcame each hardship and became wiser and stronger.

I lived an idyllic childhood in Iowa as a talented, accomplished child full of promise with sights set on The Juilliard School of Music. In the earlier years, my family lived in Madison County where the notorious historical covered bridge attracted tourists and inspired a book and a movie. I frequented that bridge as a young girl.

I remember one time, a white butterfly captured my attention. I chased it as far as I could as it fluttered along, eventually flying out of sight. I wanted to be free like that butterfly as it sailed through its life without boundaries. During my teenage years, harsh lessons taught me that freedom is hard-won, and it comes at a price. It doesn't always lead to happiness or success.

Growing up as a middle child of five and serving as lead flutist in my early years, I was primed for leadership. I played first chair in the youth symphony, marching band, and orchestra. But then life took a horrible turn.

I was in my thirties when I rebounded and orchestrated a rally that resulted in a robust, purposeful career through which I was able to impact the lives of thousands of children and families. I also raised a remarkable daughter on my own, I found love and lost love, and became the best version of myself.

Now, as a retired sixty-something woman, I contemplate my past and consider whether I have the courage and fortitude to share it. My life story is compelling and worth telling. It isn't always pretty—it is honest and raw—but I am putting it all out there. For some, this may be a hard read because I've been forthright and candid regarding my personal truths.

On a broader scale, lessons from a robust, purposeful career spent advocating for domestic violence victims and working for child welfare are also worth sharing. Those experiences reflect a side of society not normally exposed, but I share it because that time played a significant role in my rebound from the traumas of earlier years. As tough and draining as that work was, it grounded me. And because of my difficult background, I was able to relate to those I served whose lives were challenged. My career promoted a feeling that I was doing what I was born to do.

I aspire to be a positive role model for my daughter, grandchildren, and others by having an optimistic attitude and showing how to age well and lift others up who are walking through the trenches. Realizing that everything I do and say matters has fostered a call to action, which has motivated me to become a writer. I was in leadership positions for most of my career. I have learned that we all lead all day, every day by how we live.

In fact, a person can never *not* lead. By our actions, we model behavior for others.

I hope my life story will enlighten readers. I hope my grandchildren will realize that life is a complicated journey but always worthwhile. Even in the worst of times, it is a magnificent gift. I hope they know that no matter what mistakes they make, they are *enough just by being*. I hope they know that when things are at their worst, they must endure, stay the course, and carry on. I hope they learn a vital lesson—that it is often not a good idea to solve a temporary problem with a solution that has permanent consequences.

I hope they realize that although Grandma Gigi was not always a good role model, her story shows they can always believe in a brighter tomorrow. To this end, I have included a section at the end on lessons learned.

If I can help one person eliminate one heartache or encourage one person on the brink of giving up or making an unwise decision, then my candor and transparency in my story will have been worth the vulnerability. My goal now is to matter, to inspire others, and continue to make a difference in their lives. I aspire to leave this world better. To that end, I write, I share, and I hope.

SONG OF THE FLUTE

Playing the flute, the beating of my heart
Its holes I plugged to the depths of my life

Life shot its best, leaving gaping wounds
I reached for the flute and began to cover its holes
My breath became song and it began to sing

The song of love, the song of hate
Of peace and war
Of silence and clamor
Of promise and defeat
Of hope and despair
Of gain and loss

The song of my heart beating once more

I heard healing melodies
As I looked back and sighed,
You have no hold on me,
I whispered and cried

My soul rejoiced as my breath and fingers played
And a song of life rang out once more

Joan Sandergard

My story is filled with broken pieces, terrible choices, and ugly truths. It's also filled with a major comeback, peace in my soul and a grace that saved my life.

Calvin Coolidge

Chapter 1

SHE WORKS HARD FOR THE MONEY

Stage Call: "Sunshine, you're on!"

Lights dazzle, the stage is set. Pulsating music blasts. Hazy smoke fills the air. I enter a bustling club dressing room filled with brash and bedazzled women flaunting incredible cleavage, bouffant hairdos, and theatrical makeup. Preoccupied with primping in mirrors and squeezing into skimpy costumes, their enthusiasm is palpable. My stage call is imminent. I slip into a black sequin dress with spaghetti straps and slits up the sides. With red lips, long blonde hair flowing to the middle of my back, five-inch heels designed to emphasize a strut, a cheater dress tailored to accentuate curves, a body oiled to shine, and "the girls" pushed up by a skimpy, glittery bra, I am stoked and ready to go. My heart is pounding out of my chest.

"Sunshine, you're on!" the manager barks.

***

My husband died in 1978 when I was nineteen, leaving me to raise our one-and-a-half-year-old daughter alone. My immaturity and efforts to dull the pain and guilt from that loss caused me to make foolish decisions that eventually almost cost me my life. I became a dancer for money. It wasn't the money, though, that captivated me most. It was the music, the movement, the exhilaration, the escape. It was, quite simply, the dance.

When I entered the club for the first night for a trial run, I was nervous and apprehensive but strangely confident. My bag was packed with a costume and make-up. After being introduced to the owner and shown around the club, I downed a stiff drink to both psych up and numb myself for what was about to happen. I stopped to watch a girl dancing provocatively on the stage. Eyes followed me as men called out for me to take the stage. The patrons appeared harmless, or so I thought. The other dancers were welcoming and encouraging, which boosted my confidence. I was new to Houston and lonely. The prospect of friendships with kindred souls was appealing.

I stepped onto the stage with cheers and jeers from the audience, but my focus was on the dance. Pulsating music carried me away. I loved the dance. I lived for the dance. It was my time to be free—to feel, to be at one with the music as my body swayed and stimulated the audience with its rhythm.

It was good to feel something good. Since my husband's death, all I had felt was unrelenting hurt and guilt. I longed for the music to provide an escape, a distraction from painful emotions I desperately tried to bury. Also, once I relaxed into the dancing, I was good at it—really good. To me, the body movement was artful expression, and it was thrilling to feel competent at something. I was not looking to hook up with anyone, but still, I generated heat.

How did I, this modest Iowa girl from a conservative family, end up as a dancer in a Texas strip club? I moved there from Des Moines, Iowa, in 1979, a twenty-one-year-old widow with a three-year-old daughter. Although my parents and my husband's parents were doing their best to help and console me after his death, I needed to find my own way. Living in the same city where my husband Bodie died, was a painful, constant reminder of my loss. I wanted a new beginning. So, I bolted.

Running away was what I did. I was a rebellious teen. I ran several times in my life, but it was never a good fix. It generated failures that made things worse. This went on throughout my young adult years until I finally moved beyond *fix and fails* and found my footing in my thirties.

As sad as it made my parents to see me leave Des Moines, I ventured out on my own determined to become independent. I believed a fresh start in a new environment would make my life better. I had to go.

With my little girl, Angel, in tow, I drove a U-Haul from Des Moines to Houston and rented an apartment. I held tight to my little girl. We could find a new life together, I thought. My older sister lived in Houston, which comforted my parents. However, because of her busy schedule, I rarely saw her. Would things have been different if we had connected? I'll never know.

I welcomed a fresh start in a new city, but finding work with no experience was a challenge. Befriending my new neighbor proved to be a mistake. I settled into an apartment next door to this woman whose father owned a small club. A business-like person, she managed the club for him. Roxie approached me before I'd even had time to unpack all the boxes or had a chance to get a job. A manipulative, self-serving woman with a cigarette in one hand and a drink in the other, Roxie went to work on me. I had never met anyone like her before.

In retrospect, her manipulation was obvious. She preyed on my vulnerability. New in town and lonely, I was eager to start over and make friends. Also, I needed to find work and generate income to supplement the Social Security I received for my daughter. Employment options were limited.

Roxie pestered me relentlessly to try dancing. "The money is good," she said. Although she took advantage of my situation, I take full responsibility for my bad decision to accept when she persuaded me to be her guest at the club. I declined at first, but her persuasive nature prevailed. "You will be a natural at dancing," she said. "Just try it." Finally, I caved.

It was a small club, and after a few stiff drinks, I decided to give dancing a shot. One dance later, I was hooked. "Not as hard as I thought," I said to Roxie. The club patrons loved me. It seemed harmless; the money was easy, and I received encouragement from the staff and patrons. I found a wonderful lady to babysit, who had a daughter the same age as Angel. And it was on. I danced, and I danced some more.

The movement took my mind away from the weight of my world. After a simmering build-up, the lights dimmed as my dress slid off my body. The thrill from the attention and limelight were familiar from many years of childhood dance recitals, community playhouses, and musical performances on the stage as a star flutist. Stage performance was second nature to me. I was free, dancing in the night—a dancing queen. Night after night, confident and without stage fright, I slipped off my clothes, leaving only a silver sequined thong, garter, stockings, and heels. Dollar bills floated onto the stage.

Colored lights, pulsating music, the smell of whisky, and a smoke-filled room were my world. The stage was familiar. The men, well that was another matter. Men stared, and frequently asked for lap dances, which fortunately was against the club rules. The small, privately owned club had regulars and a bartender who ensured patrons behaved themselves, which gave me a false sense of security. When I left the stage, men would call me over to engage in small talk and to test my limits. I didn't want anything beyond the stage work, but club policy required interaction with the patrons. Although the attention was flattering, I just wanted to dance. I lost myself in the music and the movement.

The dance and artistic expression consumed me. The music was medicine. When losing myself in dance, everything was okay. The dance took me away. The dance set me free. The dance dulled my reality. And it healed me—until it didn't.

Sunshine was my name. I was a twenty-one-year-old lady of the night. Don't get me wrong. I was no prostitute or porn star or escort, but I could have been. I had plenty of offers. But I saw myself as only a dancer for money.

Camaraderie was strong among the dancers, although some were rougher in nature, disconnected, and likely on drugs. A seasoned, professional dancer, Jade, befriended me. Later she decided to go into nude dancing because the money was better. I tried to talk her out of it, but she had made up her mind.

One day, Jade motioned me over. Two professional-looking men had arrived who wished to go upstairs with us for an established fee. She had a propensity to evaluate men based on the caliber of their watches and assumed this would be a lucrative situation. Without hesitation, she went. I stayed behind knowing this would cross a line, and in my mind, it was unprofessional. How easy it was for girls to be caught up in the unfortunate side of the business. I warned her, "What if they're police officers?" It was a risk my friend would take. I thought, *hell no, I ain't going to jail. I'm a mom.* My moral compass promoted fear and trepidation and kept me from making such an unfortunate transition.

Days went by, nights dazzled, and men pursued. But my boundaries were set. I never dated anyone from the club. In fact, at that time, although I was single, I was hesitant to date or bring men around my home because of my daughter.

Then one night my neighbor Roxie dropped by my apartment accompanied by a male friend. He seemed to be a nice guy—someone I might date. I was lonely. *What could it hurt to meet a nice man?* After a short visit, my friend said she had to go and left me alone with the guy. I was apprehensive, but he seemed okay. He wasn't.

I was shocked when he abruptly pushed me toward the bedroom. I pushed back with my voice and body, but he didn't stop. As my strength waned, his power prevailed. I said no, I cried, I pushed—but it happened—I was raped.

Distraught, shamed, humiliated, disgusted, dazed, and utterly victimized, I wrapped myself in a blanket, marched to Roxie's apartment, and banged on the door. I shouted at her and ranted, "Why did you introduce me to this horrible person?" She claimed she had no idea he would do such a thing. *Oh, yeah, really?* I was too stunned to cry at this point, but I was livid. *Surely Roxie knew of his character.* I could never trust her again, nor could I forgive her for what she had done.

She asked, "Wanna call the police?" I recognized the insincerity of her suggestion. "God no, I don't want him coming back. He knows where I live, and I have a daughter. The police can't protect me twenty-four hours a day. This could escalate into something worse."

Roxie said she would talk to him and make it clear he was never to return. This was little consolation. Feeling defeated, I barely got back upstairs to my apartment, trembling, and scared of his return. I tried to sleep but couldn't. Nothing gave him the right that night to hurt me. The feeling of disgust was long-lived. Beyond repair, I longed to escape reality. However, for my little girl, my reason for carrying on, I pulled myself together.

This was the end of the road for me at the club. I bolted.

My passion for dancing remained. Tryouts were scheduled at a more elite club. It will be safer, I thought. It was my night; the large room was packed. Whisky-colored lights and shadows of men filtered through the smokey ambiance of the club as I entered.

When it was my time to perform, the loud music blared, colored lights flashed, and the spotlight blinded me as I took the stage. Hazy figures, some sitting, and some standing, looked on attentively. By this time, I had learned the moves. With confidence, I delivered a thrilling performance. My prior gig paid off for me. I was a pro, and I was good. The audience roared. I made it into the elite club. Celebrating my victory, I mused: *Maybe I could be a Rockette someday, although I would have to learn to keep my top on.*

Elated to score this win, I interpreted it as a step up and an opportunity to make more money. The club was exclusive and classy—if such a place could be classy—much different from my last job. High-end, well-dressed patrons filled the room, and good manners prevailed. As I walked off the stage and through the crowd one night, a man approached me and said, "What are you doing here? You don't belong here." I must have had "small-town Iowa girl" stamped on my forehead. I wanted to return his question with my own, "Who are you, and what are you doing here?" Instead, I kept walking and didn't engage. However, his words stuck with me, hovering in the back of my mind. At the time I ignored them, but his words proved prophetic.

One evening I met an appealing, interesting, professional-looking man at the club, and we hit it off. He was tall in stature, clean-cut, well-dressed, and down to earth with a touch of Southern charm. And he wore a nice watch. He stayed until closing time, and we walked out of the club together to the parking lot. It was a chilly night. He invited me to his Mercedes so we could keep warm while smoking cigarettes. The car smelled like a mix of cigarette smoke and Stetson cologne. As soon as I settled into my seat, without a word he started the car and whisked me into the darkness of the night. I had no chance to respond. *Bad decision. This cannot be good.*

"Where are we going?" He didn't respond. *Okay, let's try that again.* "Where are we going? I need to get home. I must pick up my daughter. Please take me back to my car." He gave me the silent treatment and continued to drive, creepily staring at the road ahead and driving away from town. "Where are we?" I asked, "I need to go home. I have a child."

"Just a short drive," he finally said, breaking his silence. Resigned to the fact that I was at his mercy, I gazed out of the car window at barren fields as he turned onto a dirt road and drove further into the dark night. I tried to figure out where I was and hoped he would take me back to the club soon. However, that was not to be. What happened after that would plague my mind forever. My kidnapper reached inside his jacket and pulled out a gun. Severe panic swept through my body and I froze.

With one hand on the wheel and the other holding the gun to my head, he sped down the dark road, which seemed to be all too familiar to him. I stared straight ahead, frightened, my stomach churning as I pondered: *Can I fight him off? Can I open the door, jump out, and roll? No.* But with no cars in sight and the dark night, I would get hurt and most likely shot.

My survival skills scratched to the surface. I had to be smart and play my cards shrewdly. "I need to get back to my daughter. She lost her father, she needs me." The dashboard lights revealed dark, cold eyes staring straight ahead. He didn't care. *What kind of human being is this? How can I stay alive?* In the middle of nowhere and complete darkness, I saw no escape without a bullet to my head. I interpreted his demand for immediate gratification as a matter of *do as instructed or die.* Terrified, I succumbed to his demands, while strategizing how to align myself with him—a survival tactic I had learned as a runaway in my youth.

Determined to use every persuasion and manipulation strategy I could muster, I said, "I can do this a whole lot better without a gun to my head." *If I could get him to put the gun down, maybe I could then get him to put it away.* He put it down; however, my tactics weren't working. Desperate as a last resort, I changed my strategy. *If I align myself with him, I can stay alive and eventually work my way back home.* This approach made my stomach churn but playing along was my only chance. I suggested that I could be his girlfriend. "It can be just you and me," I said, knowing the potential negative outcome of this proposal—that he would keep me for who knows how long—at least I could survive the night. I was comforted to know my daughter was with a family who would care for her until I could return. The question was, would I return?

Kidnapped, sexually assaulted, and almost left for dead, I made it through, if you can call it that. He eventually took me back to my car and didn't speak a word. Relieved, visibly shaken, and frightened of being followed, I could not get home fast enough. Calling the police was not an option. My survival mode told me I could not risk retribution. I had a daughter. I needed to protect her and her mother. What were the odds of the police finding him? And who would believe me—a dancer—over a distinguished professional man? I was free and alive. For that I was grateful. I would not report. And fearful he would find me, I bolted.

I understand why most women do not go to the authorities even though not doing so puts others at risk. Who knows how many women my kidnapper violated? But what were my choices? It was not just the shame and knowing I would not be believed that kept me from reporting. It was the fear of retaliation.

So many women are permanently scarred as I am. When we tell our stories to other women, it is shocking how often the response is "me, too." And the effects are long-lasting. To this day, I carry the burden of having been violated. I don't climb into a man's car, no matter how well I know him, without some degree of anxiety. The wounds never heal, and scars remain. Even for honorable men, my trust is elusive and hard-earned. For those reasons, most of my adult life I have been alone.

This was the end of my dancing days, which until writing this memoir was a part of my life I shared with only a few people. The dancing experience was a time of exploration and independence that came with a price. It ended in pain and defeat, and it cried out for a rally. Unfortunately, during those young adult years, I fell into a pattern of poor judgment that resulted in more fixes and failures to come.

I think about the lives of the girls out there dancing and wonder about their reasons for doing it. I worry: *Are they being hurt? Probably. Will they be able to get out?* I don't have the answer to that question. It's not a simple process and has its own dangers. I share my path and hope it sheds some light to others. I don't even fully understand my reasons for subjecting myself to that precarious environment. How a small-town Iowa girl went from the heartland to dancing on a stage in a strip joint in Houston is a simple question with a complicated answer.

What would I do? Where would I go after this harrowing incident? I knew I had to stop the madness of dancing, but how could I obtain gainful employment? *Do I put topless dancer at the top of my resume?* Although ill-prepared for a proper and noble career, I eventually carved one out. However, the path to redemption was wrought with more missteps and challenges. And this is where the heart of my story begins.

CHAPTER 2

A GIRL FROM MADISON COUNTY, FULL OF PROMISE

AN IDYLLIC CHILDHOOD

As I look back on my poor judgment as a young woman and those unfortunate and traumatic events in Houston, I contemplate how the idealistic Iowa, midwestern culture could have spawned such a vulnerable, foolish young woman. Although my early childhood was idyllic, no amount of attention, soothing, or counseling could reel me in during my teenage and early adult years. And no one knew why. Now, as I look back as an older, wiser woman, it is easy to understand my behavior and actions. I had a secret—a terrible, awful secret.

It was 1958 in Madison County, Iowa, the year of my birth. This is where the movie *The Bridges of Madison County*—a colorful representation of the charm of Iowa—was filmed. I lived in Madison County in my early childhood, however, my parents later moved to Des Moines. We frequently returned to that special place many times during my childhood where I visited the bridge featured in the movie. It was a sanctuary of sorts, a place where I could dream, run, and hide while safely ensconced in nature. On a sunny Iowa morning, the scent of wildflowers soothed me. It was there that my fascination with butterflies was nurtured. As mentioned earlier, when I chased that white one fluttering around, I wanted to be free—to sail through life without boundaries like that butterfly. I yearned to experience the spontaneity its world afforded.

As a young child, my life was idyllic—mostly. My parents encouraged my innate musical and performance talent. I excelled at playing the flute and piano as well as singing, and was active in a community playhouse, taking to the stage in various roles. I was a good student and an aspiring achiever in all aspects of my young life. With an ingrained quest to be at the top of my game, whatever the game, and a natural inclination toward ambition, I excelled at everything. When I look back, I can't recall having a sense of failure at anything as a young girl.

I eventually took to the stage as the number one flutist. My name was known throughout the city and state. Second place was not my nature, and I was rarely beaten in auditions. Competition and stage presence anchored me, taught me discipline, and gave me confidence. A star soloist, an award winner at the Iowa State Youth Symphony, in the news and in the know, my reputation followed me throughout elementary school, junior high, and a portion of my high school years. Mother planned my future at the elite Juilliard School of Music in New York City. My days were filled with practice. When I performed, the stage was mine. I owned it, and I relished the experience.

My parents were of humble means with Mom keeping house and caring for five children. Dad was a pharmacist with a strong work ethic. His career blossomed as he served on the Governor's drug abuse council for the state of Iowa. And he amassed many other outstanding achievements. A pillar of the community, he was loved by many. With Dad working long days, Mom was left at home with five young children. Sometimes he was not there for Christmas mornings or other holidays. Restless, we waited eagerly for Dad to arrive home so we could be together and open our gifts, which were limited and modest, but fully appreciated. I was so excited one year to unwrap a pair of fuzzy blue slippers, my only gift, but they were everything to me. One time I was ecstatic to get a doll from Santa. My siblings and I grew up being grateful for little things and all our parents did for us. It amazes me how much children have today and how contented we were with so little. By today's standards, my siblings and I were deprived.

Mom was a fifth-grade teacher in her early years, but with five children, that career fell by the wayside. Like Dad, she was a hard worker and masterfully managed the household. She was often seen around town pushing two strollers with other children tagging along. Her honed organizational skills and knack for budgeting were vital to living on Dad's limited income. Our food budget was tight, but Mom made it work. Borden's delivered glass milk bottles to our milk box on the front step each week. Milk was mixed with powdered milk and rationed among us. Local farmers brought sweet corn to our home in large feed bags. We kids took turns sitting at the corner selling it throughout the summer months. We rarely had salad dressings, gravy, or sauces. Mom said, "The flavor is in the vegetables." Sometimes all we had for dinner was rice and mustard greens. A full-page article published in the Des Moines newspaper reported that Mom fed a family of seven for $17.00 a week.

Mom managed to have homemade meals on the table every night. At dinner, five children competed for the center of attention and occasionally fought over a chicken leg or the last of the mashed potatoes. As we got older, we were required to bring a newsworthy article to the table and lead a discussion about it.

Pay phones, party telephone lines, and manual typewriters were modern features to us. We shopped at dime stores. Twenty-five cents a gallon gasoline was purchased with cash from stations where a man pumped gas, washed windshields, and aired up the tires.

My parents did it all: church, choir, and pancake Sundays. In winter, we made snow igloos and enjoyed sledding and tobogganing down hills. We frequented outdoor ice-skating rinks and enjoyed local college basketball games. Iowa State Fairs, tandem bicycle rides, neighborhood pig roasts, as well as gardening, picnics, and swimming at local pools were common, inexpensive activities. Family vacations to Tennessee and Kentucky in our blue Chevrolet station wagon packed with snacks, food, paper maps, and a "potty pot" were cherished adventures.

Iowa had an exceptional educational system. The standards were high, and my siblings and I studied diligently. We worked hard and played hard. This included kite flying, crafts, baking, sewing, summer camps, bike rides, neighborhood softball games, ping pong, decorating bicycles for Fourth of July parades, and riding our horses—Toby and Joe. We often hung out at the soda fountain in the pharmacy where Dad worked. Mom and Dad called family meetings in the den as needed to coordinate our activities, inform us of new rules, and convey family news.

Life was idyllic.

When I began fourth grade, girls were allowed to wear pants to school, eliminating frostbite from bitter frigid days. Home economics was mandatory for girls to learn about etiquette, how to cook and sew, and what it meant to be a girl. Shop was required for boys to teach them the trades and what it meant to be a boy. Photos and televisions were black and white, and records were 45 rpm. The Beatles and The Rolling Stones were all the rage.

Almost every generation has some kind of war or international crisis to deal with. At that time the cold war was in its prime. Russia threatened to annihilate us. People built bomb shelters in their homes and yards. Black and white, reel-to-reel, films at school told us to crawl under our desks if we saw a flash of light from an atomic bomb as if that would do us any good.

Being a middle child–an older brother and sister-two younger sisters-had its challenges, but it encouraged assertiveness, promoted leadership skills, and fostered teamwork. We all played well together with few sibling arguments. Performance was always on my agenda, and my younger sister and I frequently put on programs for the family. We kids were fortunate, and I felt secure, loved, and protected for the most part. But all was not as idyllic as it seemed. I was keeping a terrible secret.

I was closest to my older brother growing up, always his shadow. I shared a room with my older sister, who looked after me until she moved out to go to college. A sense of abandonment surfaced when she left, leaving me to sleep in our bedroom alone.

As I went through turbulent times as a teenager, I let my siblings down, and at times our relationships were strained. They couldn't understand why I behaved the way I did, yet I was sure that they would understand—if they knew my secret. Once they knew, they didn't judge me. We have disagreements but accept our differences. In recent years, as orphans after our parents died, we've learned to manage without them, which has enhanced our bonds.

We kids enjoyed time with our maternal grandparents, Grandma and Grandpa A. They lived in a small town in Iowa where family values were instilled, and we learned about our roots. Both Grandma and Grandpa A were actively involved with each one of us. It is said that grandparents contribute significantly to their grandchildren's self-esteem, and that is true in my case. They never failed to ask about our academic achievements and extracurricular activities. And they insisted I bring my flute to practice and play for them. They were stern but loving, right-and-proper people—pillars of the community who adhered closely to rigid Midwestern conventions and propriety. Their standards were high, and over the years, I occasionally fell short of them. But my belief in their unconditional love never wavered.

My grandfather had an insurance business and was an avid gardener. Grandma cooked vegetables from his garden and always had roses on the table for dinner. They loved to travel in their Airstream trailer and drove their Cadillac south each winter. Theirs was a successful loving marriage for sixty years.

I withdrew from my grandparents in earlier years, feeling I had disappointed them with my poor behavior and not fulfilling my potential as a flutist. My grandma had a stroke, and I visited her as she lay in a coma. I told her how sorry I was for my ways, that I loved her, and to please live because I needed her. I don't claim to be the reason for her recovery, but she did miraculously awake from the coma and went on to live many more productive years.

Grandpa and I became close in his later years when he was "the last man standing" in my lineage. He saw me through rough times but always believed the best in me. A believer in good penmanship, he often sent me handwritten letters. He wrote his life story in his eighties, memorized poetry into his nineties, learned to bake, and entertained the ladies in the retirement home after Grandma died. I returned to visit him often in his golden years, always taking my flute on the plane when Grandpa arranged for me to play a concert at his retirement village, proudly introducing me as his granddaughter.

Grandparents on my father's side were significantly different from my mother's. Dad was the only child of a doctor and an aristocratic, high-society, mother, Grandma E. His father owned a pharmacy. Grandma's home was full of high-end items, which made us children feel as though we were in a glass house full of untouchables. A woman full of grace and beauty, Grandma was always adorned with jewels, furs, and hats and drove a Cadillac around town. She awoke daily by 4:00 a.m. to sit at her vanity and "put on my face." By the time the rest of us woke up, she was sitting at the kitchen table with a cigarette in one hand and coffee in the other, primed, and ready to meet the day.

I never saw Grandma E without a stylish dress and her hair beautifully done from her regular trips to the beauty salon. In her earlier years, she looked like a model. She loved dressing my dad as a young boy. He had forty suits of assorted styles by the time he was four years old.

When I first brought my husband to meet Grandma E, he wore his long hair down, a characteristic of his Indian heritage. Grandma dressed him in Grandpa's white silk pajamas and told him he looked like Jesus. Grandma E was married and widowed twice. Interestingly, her second husband was a farmer—an odd combination. I became close to this elegant woman in my adult years following the death of her second husband. It was then that

I discovered something we had in common. She loved alcohol as much as I did.

I didn't know until I was much older that my father was adopted. His mother died giving birth and his father was unable to care for him and his older sister. He was placed in an orphanage and adopted by my grandmother E when he was nineteen months old.

My biological grandfather H was 100 percent Danish and one of thirteen children. He was the only one of his siblings to come to America, migrating in 1912. A WW1 vet, he served in France, later becoming a janitor who lived to be ninety-one. I was fortunate to have met him before he died. Growing up, I was sometimes called *My Little Dane* when visiting grandparents because I resembled my Danish family. This was a name originating in the Viking Age. I wonder, even today, how many unknown Danish cousins I have in that beautiful country with the reputation of being the happiest country in the world. I was proud of my Denmark heritage. *A Viking I will be.*

Family, faith, God, and country were values held high in our family. As a young child at campfire camp, I hiked my way up to what was known as a spiritual peak. It was there, in the solitude of nature, that I had an awakening and the realization of a spiritual connection—a moment in time that touched me deeply. That was a defining experience that symbolized the pleasantries of my early childhood. It was a special memory. But, as I entered my teenage years, idyllic times sank into the background as unfortunate incidents invaded my world and superseded special memories.

During my late childhood, family dynamics shifted. Mom converted to the Catholic faith. Dad went to our Protestant church on his own for a while but eventually retreated to his work desk in the basement on Sundays.

Mom was a Republican and Dad a Democrat which was never discussed in our home or viewed as a point of contention, although, it created curiosity. As Mom became more involved in her Catholic faith and preoccupied with the Parent Teacher Association and her Pi Beta Phi sisterhood, my parents drifted apart. Conflict intruded into their relationship, and a sense of insecurity and abandonment surfaced in me.

Dad was always the peacemaker in the family—a softie—and mom the disciplinarian. He occasionally got into trouble for allowing me to keep stray dogs and cats that I brought home and hid in my bathroom. When Mother found out, Dad got a chewing out. I was Daddy's girl, and I felt sorry for him when he got in trouble because of me.

Eventually, Dad's soft, quiet nature shifted, and they argued in the evenings behind closed doors after we kids went to bed. My room was close to theirs, and the arguing kept me awake. I went to school tired, frequently going to the nurse's office with my stomach in knots. As the nightly arguing and sleepless nights continued, Mother broke off pieces of her Valium to give me to help me sleep. I didn't want to take it, but she assured me it was okay. It was not okay. As the circumstances at home shifted, my world did so as well. I harbored a horrific secret, and things were about to change in a significant way.

CHAPTER 3

THE UNDERTOW OF VICTIMIZATION

A Reluctant but Determined Rebel

The sixties were formative, foundational years for me, an enthusiastic young child thriving in a world flourishing with big dreams and accomplishments. In the seventies, I turned twelve and a storm brewed that would leave devastation and destruction in its wake. This threat was so pervasive that it was as though a churning cloud hung over my head.

I missed my sister who had gone off to college. My brother was now in his preteen years and, although we were only thirteen months apart, and up until now, inseparable, he was growing into a young man. His activities took him in different directions. My anxiety continued to grow as I was left to battle sleepless nights alone, often the result of my parents' nightly arguments. I called out to them many times, asking them to lower their voices. They would do so for a few minutes, and then the verbal arguments would again kick into gear. I suffered from frustration, anxiety, and stomach aches, in addition to sleep loss. My father, the softer and calmer one of the two whom I adored, began coming into my room at night to tuck me in and lower my anxiety. However, the Valium from Mother and his calming approach were not working.

During one of Mom and Dad's arguments, I overheard them mention divorce. I begged them not to. I loved both of my parents very much, and as a child, I knew my mom would be okay, but I worried about my dad. I was happy when he came in to tuck me in. Over time, his visits to my bed lasted longer. Then, one night, everything changed....

Dad's touching, which was intended to relax me, began to shift off-center. He called it "cuddling." The cuddling increased in intensity and escalated to fondling. Dad looked for me when Mom was gone during the day and came into my room at night. He came into the bathroom when I was taking a bath to wash my back.

Every time Dad and I were alone, some form of fondling occurred, and it continued to progress. Dad's touch felt good, the first of any kind for me. He was loving and sweet, and I enjoyed the attention and even the touch. But as time went on, I somehow knew that what was happening to me was not right. My feelings changed from wanting our secret time alone to being petrified about what would happen to me if Mom were to leave. With her around, I was safe. It felt as though I was Dad's girlfriend, an awkward situation. I intuitively concluded cuddling was wrong, and I didn't enjoy it anymore. When I became determined to stop it, our relationship changed.

I felt dirty and grieved over my loss of innocence and no longer being daddy's girl. I considered telling Mom but couldn't bear the thought of hurting her or causing more problems between them. Confused and deeply disturbed, I wanted to fix the mess but didn't know how.

I wondered if Dad had a problem with sex. Did he have a girlfriend? I snuck into my parents' room trying to find answers. I discovered adult magazines under the bed on Dad's side. They left me disgusted. And I knew then where my father was headed with the cuddling, and I was petrified. I was being groomed for something greater. I wasn't going to let that happen and it didn't happen.

Sex was never discussed in my home, and there were no Sex 101 classes in school. To me, sex didn't exist until the inappropriate touching became routine. Dad's behavior and those magazines stole my innocence, and a storm brewed in my head. Hurricane winds were on the horizon, and they were going to be fierce. They would influence my life in ways I could not have imagined as a young girl.

Days, weeks, and months passed with tension building from trying to avoid Dad's inappropriate touches. My life spiraled out of control. Ambition and enthusiasm for activities—one of my most redeeming personality traits—waned. My once wide circle of friends narrowed. I struggled to keep my well-known status as the number one flute player in the district.

I became embarrassed as those who believed in me looked at me in wonder as my life spiraled downward out of control. I no longer had an interest in running for Student Council, playing on the girls' basketball team, or doing all the other things I used to enjoy. Even the passion for playing the flute evaporated. I withdrew from my friends and sought out new friends who matched how I felt inside—horrible and unworthy of accomplishment. I hung around the kids at school who smoked—the "bad kids." I was strangely comfortable there and soon found myself in cars in the school parking lot, taking drags on cigarettes, and skipping school. I partied with my new friends and began drinking alcohol around the age of fifteen. Doing so numbed my confused feelings and tempered the effects of trouble at home. I dressed differently and acted differently. With few exceptions, my parents seemed oblivious to my transformation, until....

Anger churned inside of me as I struggled to avoid Dad and mentally dealt with his actions. The loss of our connectedness burned deep. My efforts to keep him away included physically fighting with him when he tried to talk to me. I cycled deeper into a negative mental state and things became hostile. The "cuddling" and giving in to Dad didn't feel good anymore, and I made things worse by fighting with him.

The friction caused problems throughout the family. Mom and my siblings were mystified by my puzzling behavior. The situation became intolerable. I didn't feel safe. Something had to change.

Finally, I rebelled against my father's abuse and bolted. I packed my bag and ran away.

Determined to survive on my own, I persuaded a friend to run away with me, not knowing where we would go or how we would get there. My friend suggested a place where we could stay with older guy friends. We hitchhiked out of town to their place. Fearful of trouble for harboring underage kids, they soon kicked us out. I had no place to go. So, I returned home.

This didn't go well with my parents. Rules got stricter, my rebel nature intensified, and friction in the home increased. Again, I ran.

This time I found a friend who had money to run with me. She got us a room out of town at a motel. We were happy on our own. She told her aunt where we were, assuring me her aunt would not tell her parents. Fifteen minutes later, the police knocked on our door. We were taken to jail to wait for our parents to pick us up. Alone, in a cold, barren cell, I thought, *this is, no doubt, not going to be fun.*

I felt shame but held on to defiance. No one asked me why being at home was intolerable, nor did anyone offer to help me. I continued to keep my secret.

With no explanation for my behavior, I was labeled another bad kid to lock up, so I didn't cause any more trouble. I wished they knew I was not a bad kid. I was just trying to get away from something bad. I sought protection and safety. I was a promise child and should have been in the papers with my many accomplishments: winning music contests, performing, and becoming the number one flutist in the state. Instead, I was in jail.

My friend's parents picked her up in a reasonable time. My parents, who were determined to teach me a lesson, let me spend the night in jail. I was as confused by my behavior as everyone else. Mother picked me up the next morning and spoke not a word the whole way home. It was a long drive.

There was no discussion when we got home either. No one acknowledged the situation, and life soon returned to the way it was before I ran away and landed in jail.

With no conversation about the problems, no solutions, and no counseling, I became the scapegoat in an environment with rigid rules, severe tension, and broken relationships.

Running away was no longer an option. It was a solution with a poor outcome. Although the "cuddling" had subsided, I was determined not to let it happen again—ever. But I felt damaged. I turned to drugs as an escape, or at least to dull the pain. I played *if only* games in my head and, with no answers, got deeper and deeper into trouble. *If only they hadn't argued. If only I had the room at the opposite end of the house. If only I wasn't a light sleeper, if only, if only....*

I had a party with my new friends in my parents' basement one night when they were gone. They raided my dad's pharmaceutical drug samples. Was he ever mad. I had grievously wounded my father, a member of the Drug Abuse Council for the Governor of Iowa. My parents' angel child had become their worst nightmare—a terror. My new friends were wild. Although the fun distracted me from my problems, hanging with them was foolish. A friend was drugged and then raped at one of the parties. I had begged to be left alone and escaped the horror. I kept this a secret for many years, blaming myself for her rape.

During this time, I was introduced to opiates and often given pills—with no idea what they were. They came with the promise that they would make everything better. Better was what I needed; however, I didn't know that combining alcohol and pills was not a good idea. After a night of taking both, I managed to make it home from the party but slept for two solid days. I faintly heard my parents talk on the phone about me not waking up, and they took me to a hospital. There was no more fight left in me. So, I went. Everything I tried to kill the anguish inside of me hadn't worked.

Once admitted to the adolescent unit for treatment, I would not speak. I was given a pill but spit it out after the nurse left. I was not going to take a pill that I didn't know why I was taking it, which was an irrational thought given the array of street drugs I had been taking. I also believed there was nothing wrong with me. *If they knew what I had been through, they might find me smart. I always got good grades, and I was, by God, known by name, as the best flutist in town of all my peers.*

I fought with the staff on purpose to get myself put into isolation, so I didn't have to be around the other people who were in treatment. The doctor tried to talk to me, but I didn't speak a word. Neither did he, as I sat silent in my chair until dismissed. I had a secret I had kept for a long time, one too complicated, hurtful, and embarrassing to tell.

I received cards and well-wishes from my siblings, neighbors, and family friends. I was not sick, so the compassion created confusion. I did appreciate that people cared, but I was embarrassed and unable to explain. *If only they knew why.*

No one ever asked me why I ran away, took drugs, and misbehaved. The doctor didn't even ask why as he sat quietly in his chair staring at me. I cannot help but wonder, as I look back, what might have happened if someone had. Why did I have a drastic, immediate change of behavior and a personality change? Why had I suddenly begun making bad choices? And why did I not want to be at home?

While sitting in the hospital, collecting all those good wishes, and contemplating my situation, I couldn't help but think it was my parents who needed help, not me.

When the time came for me to go home, I refused. I could not run away, nor fight my dad. Neither of those had worked out before. Drugs and alcohol got me in a lockdown unit. I could not tell my secret, and I could not stay at home. Every solution I tried had not worked, and I continued to be in a fix. My options were laid out in front of me. I could go to a girls group home, a foster home, or go home. None of these sounded good to me. *At least jail is not an option.*

I wanted the freedom to sail through life like the white butterfly I once chased at the covered bridge. Instead, I felt as if I were free falling with no safety net. I had a good solid upbringing. Early on, my father was loving, caring, and nurturing. Dad was intelligent, had a good sense of humor, and was always in my corner. I could not have asked for a better father, until I didn't have one anymore.

I had lost my father. As a result, it was as though I was unanchored. I learned survival skills, became street smart, and evolved into a formidable young woman—a fighter. This...my dad taught me. I was determined not to go back home. I refused to experience the friction and tension there. My decision to take a stand reflected a turning point. I fought for something better.

Because of Dad's betrayal, I would never feel safe at home. I grieved that loss intensely, but with the naivety of youth, I believed what happened was my fault. I didn't realize that guilt was the motive for much of my behavior. What had happened was no little thing. It caused me to lose everything, but it taught me to be strong and stand up for myself. I was given a choice of where to go. I chose, of my own free will, to go into a foster home. Although only a temporary reprieve, it was just the medicine I needed. It was time for self-care.

Against all odds, I hit the jackpot when it came to the foster home I was given. I learned years later while working for a state child protection services agency the rare good fortune I had experienced because of the family I was placed with. Their approach to caring for me during this time was exceptional. This was a crucial turning point in my life, a defining time that made all the difference. It is not an exaggeration to say that this family saved me. The feeling of free falling subsided. I felt safe. Still, the road to recovery was far from over and it took years to repair the damage to my psyche that clung to me like gum in my hair.

CHAPTER 4

FOSTERING HOPE

AN ANGEL TO THE RESCUE

I found the answer to my situation with my newfound foster family. No longer would I feel like a problem child in an unbearable situation. I knew my choice would hurt Mom, but survival was my top priority. And I couldn't bear to tell her what was happening with Dad, as that would hurt her greatly. It could cause a divorce that would be my fault. I had to leave.

In foster care, I was surrounded with seven siblings, including five biological children, one special needs foster brother, and an older lady they took care of who was born with no arms or legs. Her limbs extended only to her elbows and knees, but she went up and down the stairs, scooted herself around, got in and out of bed, crawled into her chair at the dinner table, and was self-sufficient in every way. She stayed in her room most of the time and rarely left the house. I asked her what she did with her time. She said reading occupied her days. An amazing, inspirational person, she influenced me in a positive way. She taught me gratitude and overcoming, lessons that made an impression and served me well in years to come.

My foster mother was an angel. I liked her right off. She worked hard taking care of her family. She bought me new clothes. Accustomed to wearing hand me downs from my sister, wearing new clothes was overwhelming initially. *Do I deserve them?* I adjusted quickly, though. I also liked and admired my foster father. Their generous support of the three fosters in their home was remarkable. I was fortunate to have landed there, and I knew it.

Mealtime consisted of the whole family around the table with good homemade food and nightly after dinner chores. I rotated between sweeping floors, helping with dishes, and putting away the food. I enjoyed the generous meals which were often lacking in my home due to finances.

I thought about my family often, but believed they were better off without me. I eventually opened up to my foster mother about why I didn't want to go home. She was my hero, the only person in my life who asked me why I didn't want to go home. Social services were involved, and they occasionally came to the home; however, they didn't speak with me. I didn't know at the time that my parents were meeting with them. Soon enough I found out. *Finally, someone to help them*—or so I thought.

Although things were going well at the foster home, life at a new high school was rough with numerous adjustments and awkward efforts to make new friends. I stayed to myself and avoided alcohol and drugs for the most part. I wanted to be good and worked hard to normalize my behavior. Unfortunately, I developed a crush on my foster brother, and we got caught smoking marijuana. My foster parents treated me as if I were their own, and they kept me despite my transgression. I took accountability and accepted the resulting punishment. I had respect for them and was grateful they gave me another chance. It was amazing all they did to help me, especially with their own children to take care of.

Walking home from school one day, I was stopped by a man who wooed me into his RV by offering me pretty dresses. Falling for convincing promises,

I reluctantly went into the trailer. He told me about how he could make my life better and promised me he would take care of me and buy me pretty clothes. He showed me a notebook with pictures of girls dressed in beautiful dresses. He gave me a hard sell with what I soon concluded were empty promises when my intuition finally kicked in. Going away with a stranger scared me, and I realized *I had been tricked*. I dashed out of the trailer and ran home. I could not get there fast enough. As I look back, I realize I was being recruited for sex trafficking and how lucky I was he didn't shut the door and take off with me.

Most of my time was spent with school, family chores, band activities, and being around home. Although externally I was okay, I could not shake an all-consuming internal anxiety. I suffered from considerable emotional pain. One day I took a cigarette and burned myself on the wrist on purpose to alleviate the feelings of shame and guilt that everything that had happened was my fault. Faint scars from this remain to this day and serve as a reminder of the battles I fought and won. I was not suicidal, but I know now that I should have been in counseling. At least I was no longer numbing my feelings with alcohol and drugs or running away from home.

After six months in the foster home, I was told my parents were taking me out, and I had to return home. My placement in the home was voluntary on my part and with their consent. To resolve my running away problem, they had agreed to let me go into foster care and were now able to reverse that placement. The prospect of going home was deeply disturbing, and I became incredibly sad and anxious. The trust that I would be safe there had been shattered, and I was embarrassed to be with my siblings whom I believed would surely resent what I had done to the family. I talked with my foster mother about my fears. I wanted to stay with her. In my mind, this was my family now. I could not live in my biological parents' home. Forcing me back was terribly wrong.

For the first time, I met with someone from the social services agency. My parents were lobbying them hard to get me back, and the social worker told me I had to go home. I insisted that I couldn't go home. She said I had no choice; I had to go. Again, I told her I couldn't. A discussion pursued and, finally, I told her why. My foster mother had prepared me for this. She advised me that I would need to tell the social worker and offered love, support, and encouragement as I came to understand why.

Once advised of the situation, the social worker insisted I meet with my parents. She would be present at the encounter when I tell my father that if I came home, the "cuddling" had to stop. I begged her not to make me do it, but she insisted. It was hard enough to disclose that to my foster mother and the social worker but telling my parents would take all the fortitude I could muster. Everything within me resisted. Did social services not believe me? Why was I the one to tell? I was frightened and anxious.

When the time came to meet, I felt awkward and uncomfortable seeing my parents when I walked into the room. My mother appeared put out. She gave me *the look*—you know, the one only a mother can give that permeates every cell in a child's body. The social worker spoke briefly, but I heard nothing she said. Then she nodded at me, and I knew it was my turn. With every ounce of strength, I faced my father for the first time and told him if I came home, the "cuddling" had to stop. I didn't dare look at my mother's face. I could only imagine her shock. But as she always did, she remained stalwart throughout the meeting. My father agreed, as if it was not a big deal. His defense was that he was just trying to relax me so I could sleep. Shortly thereafter, with no further discussions or questions, I went home.

Somehow in the back of my mind I thought this was a new beginning and was willing to try it—until I was given strict rules that were punitive and unbearable. I thought coming home would involve forgiveness and a fresh start. I did fine at my foster family's home without harsh rules. I had been traumatized by my father's actions and didn't believe I deserved to be punished.

I needed and wanted to be welcomed home with open arms. I needed love and forgiveness, not just for me. Everyone in my family needed healing. I was astute enough to know that I was not the only one who misbehaved in this situation. Like an immature child, my self-talk said, "You started it," referring to my dad.

I returned to my old school. Arrival and departure times were to be documented and signed by the school, which I found embarrassing. Numerous other rules that I thought were unreasonable for my age were instigated. Still, I hoped everything would be okay eventually.

Dad stopped "cuddling," but there was a breach in our relationship. And I had hurt all my family members with my behavior. We all needed support, but there was no counselor or social worker. I didn't feel loved and saw no hope for redemption. No one explained or discussed anything with me.

I got no apology from my father nor any acknowledgement of what happened from my mother. Their refusal to express regret ate at me.

Children have an intuitive sense of injustice, and I knew I had been violated. However, children also tend to blame themselves when terrible things happen to them. That induces shame. I had no idea how to cope or what to do in this situation. I was whipped.

Uncomfortable at home, particularly around my father, the atmosphere was tense. He stayed distant from me, and we avoided conversation. Mother and I never talked about what had happened until later in my adult life, although I know it changed the trajectory of her life and her relationship with her husband. My siblings' lives had gone on without me, and I had no idea of the knowledge they had about my situation. They were busy with their activities. I had missed out on their changes during the time I was gone. I tried to reestablish myself as a member of the family, but the situation remained strained and awkward.

Although I had not kept up with the flute or lessons for a couple of years, I enrolled in band. But having fallen behind, I struggled to catch up, and I was embarrassed to face my band teacher. It was mortifying when I tried out for seats and landed in second chair. This had never happened since I started playing the flute. This distressed me more than anything; it was a severe loss. I was at the height of my flute career when my father made the biggest mistake of his life and tried to "relax me." His actions and my reactions hurt both my parents and me in material ways. People can say they are sorry, but scars remain. I didn't get any "I'm sorries." Nor did I give them. Life just went on.

I was sixteen years old and a junior in high school. I had a few friends, some from my former groups, but I kept to myself at school. With transportation an issue, a friend and I decided to hitchhike our way back from a friend's house one day and were picked up by a man about four years older than we were. He liked my friend, and they hit it off and started dating. He had a good friend he wanted me to meet. Hesitant and anxious about what would be in store for me after all my previous troubles, I initially resisted the suggestion. But as my adventurous spirit kicked in, I agreed to meet for a blind date.

As I opened the door to my parents' home, I was greeted by the most gorgeous six-foot tall, long dark-haired, exotic hunk I had ever laid eyes on. I knew instantly things were going to get better—way better. My second angel had arrived.

CHAPTER 5

A SEVENTIES MAN

A FREE BIRD MEETS A FLUTTERING BUTTERFLY

In the spring of 1975, love saved me. I could abandon integrating my previous rebel self back into my family because love happened. My love, Bodie, and I worried about how to tell my parents we wanted to marry.

Bodie was the nicest person I had ever known—sensitive, caring, devoted, and honest. But I was seventeen, a junior in high school, and he was three and a half years older. Our relationship had a rocky start because I lied to him about my age. He was upset when he found out. We had a brief cooling off time after that; however, our love was strong, and it continued to blossom.

His thick, long, straight, dark hair reflected his Native American heritage, and I was in love with his exotic look. His hair, which was his trademark, was beautiful and so fitting for his olive complexion, massive stature, and chiseled and masculine features. Our relationship progressed swiftly and urgently. We were in love. Soul mates destined to journey together through life. There was no separating us. We would marry.

"There is only one way to do this," I told him. "We go to my parents together and write in the day we are to wed on their calendars." And that is what we did. My parents' reaction was probably one of relief at this point. They could turn the responsibility of me over to someone else. They accepted our love and adjusted to the idea that I would marry before finishing high school. We spoke with his parents by phone, and they were overjoyed with the prospect their son would settle down and have a family. And so, it was.

My parents' acquiescence with my getting married at the age of seventeen and before finishing high school was unusual back then. I didn't *have to get married* due to a pregnancy, as many young girls that age were expected to do, but my parents had their reasons for supporting my choice. Maybe I was a hurtful reminder of Dad's error in his ways, or it caused undue stress on their relationship. My "secret" was not revealed to Mom prior to my parents pulling me out of the foster home. Perhaps that revelation generated regrets, and they were ready to put the whole thing behind them by letting me go. No doubt, my parents viewed my relationship with Bodie and the proposed marriage as a solution. They welcomed Bodie into their home and let loose of the tight rein. We had their blessing.

Even with all my issues, I wasn't just marrying Bodie to escape an unpleasant situation. I adored him. He brought joy into my life. I wanted to do better and always looked forward to the end of the school day when he picked me up in front of the school in his van. *No more feeling embarrassed. I have an exotic hunk driving me around.* I was proud of him. He was supportive of my flute activities, attended performances, and always came to the house nicely dressed. He was proud of me and though he knew about the situation with my father, he didn't judge him or let it prevent him from developing a relationship. This touched my heart because I loved my dad very much; however, it was a confusing love. He had hurt me, and I had hurt him in return.

Bodie integrated easily into my family. Mom and Dad embraced him and invited him over for family dinners. My siblings loved him as well. He was everything to me. He had a good heart and was respectful to me, my mother, his mother, and women in general. Our hormones, no doubt, sang together in harmony creating love under the stars. We enjoyed just *being*—hanging out, passionate kisses, long talks. Our relationship was easy and developed organically without effort. It was filled with love, tranquility, and joy. Marriage was inevitable.

We picked out our rings together. He was proud to be able to give me an engagement ring with a diamond in it. It was 1975, and the engagement ring and bands cost $250. He loved his ring, which had diamond chips in it. To celebrate our engagement, family and friends planned a bridal shower, a special event where they lavished gifts and good wishes on us.

It was August 1975. I was seventeen years old. On a sizzling summer day in Des Moines with roses in full bloom, I walked into a rose garden offering a colorful display of stunning colors to join hands with the one I loved. Surrounded by a field of flowers, my sister by my side and my flute teacher playing her flute, I carried a bouquet made by my grandmother from her rose garden as I walked down the aisle on my father's arm. I wore a long white dress and a veil my foster mother purchased. Bodie wore a white jacket with white slacks and a boutonniere. I beamed as I came down the aisle. The pastor from my childhood church officiated the wedding and gave a blessing. We confessed our love for each other and exchanged rings. My love and I wrote our vows, so special and meaningful to us, and we became one. Together we celebrated with family and friends at a simple, yet perfect, reception provided by my parents. We didn't have a honeymoon but enjoyed a stay on our wedding night at an upscale hotel. It was our special day. It couldn't have been more perfect.

We set up house in a small but nice apartment and adopted a cat. I didn't know how to cook. When my cooking failed, Bodie said it was okay. He knew how to make eggs, peanut butter sandwiches, macaroni and cheese, and the best omelets. Bodie was between jobs, and we received food stamps, lived off his unemployment check, and enjoyed the many household gifts we received. For the first time in my life, I accumulated material possessions, and that was exciting. In a way, it was as though we were playing house. Despite all the blessings, after being in survival mode for three years, I didn't know how to make a home, but I would learn.

I entered my senior year in high school the following month with everyone at school wondering where I found my new hunk. I struggled with the demands of school while striving to be a good wife. Because of my age and being away from home and my mother for much of my youth, I was ill prepared for the role. This put me at a considerable disadvantage. I was embarrassed that I didn't know how to make nice dinners. I loved learning to cook when I was a young girl but had not made anything in several years. I didn't have the confidence to try Mom's special lasagna or to accumulate a collection of recipes. It was always special when Dad invited us over for grilled hamburgers and hot dogs.

I also didn't know what colors go together in the washing machine, and I ruined a few of Bodies' clothes. I had no idea how to keep a checkbook or a budget, to care for a car, or any of the many other capabilities needed in adulthood. I had not received any counseling throughout youthful traumas, had no physical relationships other than with my father, and was unprepared for sex. I made many mistakes through it all, but Bodies' love for me was strong. He was patient, supportive, and never let my inadequacies bother him. I am certain that at times he found my faux pas entertaining, but he never mentioned them or teased me.

My parents took a liking to Bodie. We visited them often. My mother taught me a lesson about marriage. I was dreamy, naive, and barely seventeen, thinking everything would be wonderful every minute of the day. Our first disagreement led me back to my mother for help, only to experience the "You made your bed, now lay in it" concept. And so, I did.

Life was full of challenges; however, we met them as they came along, certain about nothing else but our forever love. We enjoyed getting to know each other: favorite songs, interests, foods, and philosophies of life. He played the guitar. His favorite song was *Turn! Turn! Turn!* by the Byrds. Second to this, was *Free Bird* by Led Zeppelin, which he learned to play expertly on his guitar. He loved *feeling free.* We were both free spirits in a sense. My dream as a little girl sitting at the special bridge had come true. I was experiencing the flight of the butterfly.

Bodie was creative—a talented artist and poet. Most often his music, art, and poetry were about his love for me, but occasionally about himself. I dreamed about what it would be like for us to grow old together, but he said he was not going to grow old. He didn't have an explanation for this belief. It was something he seemed to know. This upset me. *We were going to grow old and be in rocking chairs together.* I didn't want to be a widow—to be without him. I cast his notion off as strange, thinking *surely not.* But I did wonder if he had a psychic sense of some sort. Or could this notion be some sort of self-fulfilling prophecy? Either way, it was disconcerting.

A few months into my senior year, Bodie was offered an incredible job opportunity in Toledo, Ohio, with Sun Oil Company. The offer included a high salary and was too good to turn down. It was time to go. So, we did. We packed everything we owned into his van, said goodbye to my parents, and moved to Ohio. We set up house there, and I found myself able to afford anything I wanted. It was great fun to shop for groceries and buy anything without hesitation. After all the years of frugality growing up, I felt like a kid in a toy store. We made friends and acquired two dogs, a bird, a rabbit, and a white cat that I found at the laundromat and brought home as I so often did as a child. I loved animals, and Bodie didn't mind. He wanted me to be happy. All the critters got along, played together, and slept together. We were happy and very much in love. Life was good.

Soon after we moved, I began to wake up with repeated episodes of morning sickness. My calculations and assumptions were correct. At the ripe old age of seventeen, I was pregnant. We were overjoyed. As a naive teenager, I had bought off on ridiculous teenage talk that it would take five years to get pregnant. So, I was not on birth control when we married. Sex education was not *a thing* back in the day. We were going to have a honeymoon baby. I immediately gave up alcohol and cigarettes for my child's sake. Bodie, filled with joy and anticipation, was especially attentive to me. It was a girl, due around my eighteenth birthday. I couldn't have been happier. Now I would have someone who would *always be mine*. I was going to have a little girl.

Life was challenging with numerous adjustments, but I had already met many challenges and, having a life partner, a sense of peace and contentment I'd not experienced before set into my soul. I enrolled in a new school for my senior year of high school, pregnant and showing. I knew everyone thought we had to get married, but I didn't care. I focused on my schoolwork and my husband with no thought of making friends at the new school. Goal oriented, I focused on getting my high school diploma, and then I would have a baby.

Bodie and I adjusted to our marital roles. He thrived at his job, and I eagerly embraced wifely duties. I loved being a wife and homemaker. I enjoyed cooking, and with my Betty Crocker cookbook, I finally learned to be a good cook. I prided myself on having a different homemade meal on the table every night for my husband when he came home from work. I even tried my hand at baked Alaska and made amazing full-course dinners. He packed a lunch bucket daily with leftovers. His co-workers were envious as the aroma of Bodie's lunch filled the break room. We also adapted socially, made new friends, and enjoyed socializing with other couples.

As wonderful as everything was, I didn't anticipate how much I would miss my mom and family. Bodie and I had worked hard at patching things up with them and they all adopted Bodie. Before we moved away, we often went to my parents' home for dinner. Those were special times, and I enjoyed seeing my husband and father laughing and joking around together. Everyone loved my husband. I became homesick and wanted to see Mom. I missed out on a relationship with her during my youth and now that one was forming, I wanted to be with her. I went home for a short visit and returned to Ohio with an even stronger desire to be near my family.

Life journeyed on. We enjoyed camping trips with friends and had other good times. Bodie was happy with his career. His mother and stepfather were local, and we visited them often. As much as Wanda, my mother-in-law, tried to make up for the absence of my mother, it was not the same. She was different from me, and her advice was sometimes questionable. She once told me I should wrap myself in Saran Wrap and lay naked under the tree on Christmas morning. This was not something I would do, nor was it something my mother would ever suggest.

Bodie told me stories about his stepfather's heavy drinking, and how the man sometimes abused his mother. One night when we were camping in a tent under the stars, he opened up about the time he went after his stepfather with a baseball bat to get him off his mother. I was shocked and saddened to hear the stories of domestic violence, an element of life with which I was unfamiliar. The only physical aggression or heavy drinking in my home was my own. My husband had been exposed to domestic violence as a young boy. Both he and his mother were affected in ways I didn't understand.

Bodie reveled in our love but occasionally showed a mysterious dark side. It had nothing to do with me. Rather, it was somehow related to his past. I couldn't make sense of his frame of mind. On those rare occasions when the quiet, dark mood overcame him, he clung to me while I simply sat with him in the dark until it subsided, which it always did. And we went on—happy and deeply in love.

Adventurous, and perhaps even foolish, we took a trip to Clingman's Dome, a popular climb among robust, athletic people in the region. Located in Tennessee, it is the highest point in the Smokey Mountains and the third highest east of the Mississippi. With an elevation of 6,643 feet above sea level, it was a steep, challenging climb with a gradient of 13%. We loved the outdoors—hiking, camping in a tent, and sleeping under the stars in Tennessee—always with creeks nearby where we could hear the bubbling water that chilled Bodie's six pack. With my doctor's permission, we undertook the challenge of climbing the dome. Although I was eight months pregnant, we climbed together, with short stops along the way so I could catch my breath. With a sense of accomplishment and the thrill of having reached the top, Bodie circled his arms around me and my baby belly as we stood there admiring a breathtaking 360-degree view spanning the Smokey Mountains and multiple states. Having accomplished this together, we had a sense we could do anything to which we set our minds.

Cruising down the highway in his van—windows rolled down, long hair flying in the wind, and Led Zeppelin playing on the radio—Bodie was a seventies man. We stopped along the way to skinny dip in Lake Erie or made our own music in the back of the van, under the stars or anywhere else our hearts desired. We were young, we were in love, and we were free. "Free as a bird," as Bodie would say, or "free as a butterfly," as I interpreted the word. It was the best time of our lives.

A week after we returned home from our climb, I felt labor pains and called the doctor. He said it was a false alarm but soon thereafter, in the middle of the night, I was certain I had lost all control. Embarrassed, I woke up Bodie and told him I had wet the bed. We called the doctor and learned my water had broken. *It is not time. It's too early, and I am still seventeen. I am not ready. I have not graduated from high school and my doctor is on vacation.*

And although we did Lamaze classes together, I was not mentally prepared for what lay ahead. I was rushed to the hospital in labor. It was nothing like I imagined or was prepared for. With Bodie by my side journaling the event, I went through the birth of our beloved daughter. It was no easy task. Stuck for hours with slow, stagnant labor, I became delirious and advised my husband I was leaving the hospital and going home. He didn't laugh, although he probably should have. I'd had enough fun, and this was not working. He and the nurse talked me into staying, of course, and we continued the childbirth journey together. Seventeen hours later, I suddenly advanced rapidly and was taken into delivery. With great pain and a body not ready for childbearing, I gave birth to our beautiful daughter.

The baby increased my desire to be near my mother—to share my child and my experiences as a mother with her. The desire overwhelmed me and transformed our lives. I should have calmed my anxiety, bucked up, adapted, and stayed the course. Instead, my restlessness changed the trajectory of our lives.

CHAPTER 6

FROM HALCYON DAYS TO CALAMITY

PUMMELED BY DEMONS FROM THE PAST

My baby girl was born with the umbilical cord wrapped around her neck. She didn't cry or make a sound and was quickly taken away after her birth. It was a difficult delivery with forceps and a frantic, resolute effort on my part. The doctor was concerned. I knew something was wrong when our daughter was not immediately laid on me and, instead, was whisked away by nurses. I became frantic with concern. *Where did she go? What is wrong? Why can't I see her?* Not a word was said. With no answers, I was a wreck. My husband tended to me until I was stabilized from the birth and then went to check on her.

He reported back that her weight was lower than projected due to arriving two weeks early, and she was jaundiced and having difficulty breathing. I was unable to hold her. Frightened and alarmed, I repeatedly begged to see her. She was given oxygen and incubated for twenty-four hours before I was finally allowed to briefly hold her. She was beautiful. I was in awe of her. Soon, someone took her away and returned her to the nursery. She remained there for seven days. Both she and I took longer than usual to recover. Distressed because I couldn't hold her, I visited her in the nursery and sat at the window for long periods of time looking at her. Onlookers commented on what a beautiful baby she was.

She truly was beautiful—like an adorable, precious little doll, perfect in every way. Bodie and I went back and forth for a few days about what to name her until I knew it had to be Angel. Bodie liked that name and immediately agreed. He always "geared to me," wanting me to be happy. The day finally arrived to take Angel home. After seven days in the hospital, we were both released. We took our baby home and eagerly began our lives together as a family.

I had purchased a pink, ruffly dress to take her home in and was excited to dress her. It was as though I had a little doll to play with. Although happy and relieved that we were both okay, I was nervous and fearful I would do something wrong. She seemed so fragile and tiny that I was even afraid to change her diaper. Back then, diapers were made of white cotton cloth with diaper pins. I was scared that with the slightest move I might hurt her. I had not practiced pinning a diaper on a tiny little human. Delighted to take over, her daddy changed the first diaper and gave her the first bath before we left the hospital.

We were new parents and had no idea what we were doing, but Angel had devoted, loving parents determined to help her thrive. We had spent months eagerly preparing for her arrival. Her nursery was decorated in a Winnie the Pooh theme. Her closet was full of pink, frilly dresses, ruffled bloomers, beautiful hand-crocheted blankets, white lacy booties, and matching bonnets. She was my precious little doll and her daddy's little princess.

My high school graduation quickly approached after we arrived home from the hospital. I was overweight, not myself, and didn't want to go through with the ceremony. But with my husband's encouragement and unwavering support, I attended the graduation ceremony with my head held high and received a high school diploma. Graduating a few weeks after giving birth with no friends in my class and knowing I was falsely and harshly judged because of my pregnancy, was one of the hardest things I had ever done. Bodie, however, was over the moon with pride as he wrapped his arms around me afterward.

Looking back while writing this today, I smile. I realize how blessed I was with such a devoted husband and a sweet, new baby. And I am proud of the courage, tenacity, and determination I demonstrated at the youthful age of seventeen. I had conquered worries about what those around me thought. I had overcome numerous challenges at such an early age—some of them with unfortunate consequences for a young girl. I had no high school proms, no promise of a future with high school reunions, and no high school friends to share life experiences with. But graduating was one of my proudest moments—a significant accomplishment after attending three different high schools and walking through the hurricane winds of my youth.

My husband and I took turns getting up with our baby in the middle of the night, but I quickly found her inconsolable. I called my mother, "Please come. I am worn out and feeling inadequate." She came to Ohio and helped me gain confidence in how to care for our baby. We soon discovered that Angel had colic. As hard as it was, I learned to lay her in the crib with her music mobile on to cry it out when we had done all we could to calm her.

Mom returned to Iowa, and I soon found myself sinking into postpartum depression. I had gained forty pounds during the pregnancy. Overweight and unable to fit into my clothes and exhausted from lack of sleep, I struggled. Once again, Bodie rescued me with unwavering love and support. He boasted of his love for me and loaned me his shirts to wear. Eventually, the hormones subsided, and my emotions stabilized.

I began a rigid regimen of restricting food intake and in six weeks was feeling back to my old self while sitting by the swimming pool in a white bikini, my baby in tow. We were inseparable, my baby girl and me.

Life transitioned into a "new normal." Once the colic was gone, Angel was a happy baby, interacting with us, cooing, and smiling. Our animals loved the new addition to our family. But for me, deep down, something was missing—my family. Bodie's mother wanted to take over rather than help me as my mother did. Mom taught me skills and boosted my confidence. My mother-in-law did the opposite. She intruded, criticized, and wanted too much time with my daughter, most likely to fill a need in her life. I never did bond with her. She told me it was my fault the cord was wrapped around our baby's neck—that it was because I did too much walking. I told her the doctor said I could walk. She also insisted I get rid of my cat, or it would smother our baby. So, I did.

Bodie worked long hours at Sun Oil with a lot of overtime. I was lonely. I had everything I could have wanted, including a devoted husband who was a good provider and the best daddy ever. But it wasn't enough. I missed my mom, my family, and my hometown. Discontentment festered. I wanted to go home, back to my Iowa roots.

I talked to my husband about this and within a year of my daughter's birth, we returned to Iowa and rented a house in Des Moines. I was much happier there, close to Mom and family. I loved keeping house and prided myself in my role as a homemaker and young mother. I hand washed cloth diapers and hung them out to dry on a clothesline in the yard. The dogs had a fenced yard with a litter of pups on the way. All was well except Bodie could not find work. He went on unemployment and searched for job opportunities with no success. Determined to remain hopeful, he persevered and diligently looked for jobs every day. But he had no luck. This weighed heavily on him, and as hope faded, his mood darkened. I felt a sense of defeat. Bodie sank into despair and guilt gnawed at me, *I had caused this to happen*. An angry dark cloud hovered over us—churning and threatening.

We celebrated our daughter's first birthday in Des Moines with my family, Bodie's father and stepmother, and others who helped make it a joyous day of celebration. Bodie decorated two homemade cakes with Winnie the Pooh on top of both. They were exceptional and reflected his amazing artistic talent.

We had a small, cute house, and I loved keeping it nice. One day we came home and saw someone crawling into one of the windows. Bodie was livid. He got our German shepherd, and with rifle in hand, snuck into the alley to hunt him down. "Do not kill him," I shouted. He didn't say a word. He eventually returned, clearly pleased with himself. That was my Bodie.

We had nestled into a predominately black neighborhood and were one of two white households on the street. We were accepted by our neighbors, and I liked them all and enjoyed the community spirit. I had a sense that those nearby "watched over us" as they knew we were in the minority. I always saw people's hearts and not their skin color. So, I was comfortable in the black neighborhood. And I adored our modest home.

More days went by, and Bodie still could not find work. This weighed heavily on him and increased my anxiety about wanting to return to

Iowa. *Had we made the right decision to move?* We once had everything
we wanted. Now we had to be more careful about finances. Bodie's
unhappiness increased. One day he suggested I could make a good living
as a banquet waitress and take care of myself and our daughter. He knew
I had worked as a banquet waitress at the top of the Holiday Inn in
downtown Des Moines the summer before my senior year. I could line
an impressive number of plates on my arms and expertly carry weighted
trays of beverages. I made top dollar working white-linen banquets and
serving high-end patrons. I never understood why Bodie said that, and he
didn't explain. Communication when things weren't going well was not
our forte. I didn't know how to climb the wall between us.

His comment concerned me. It reminded me of the one he had made when
he said he would never grow old. I couldn't make sense of such remarks,
and he refused to talk about them. His pride had suffered a great loss, and
I worried. *Is he upset because he thought I could make more money than he
could now? Or is he blaming me for the move? More worrisome: is he thinking
he will not be here in the future to take care of us?* Whatever was going on
with him, we didn't talk about why he said what he said. His mood hovered
like an angry poltergeist throughout much of our time together after the
move. During moments of delight, I relished the thought that everything
would be okay. Then the dark cloud would again hover over us, churning
as the sky darkened.

Bodie eventually got a job at a painting company at a fraction of what he
was paid in Ohio. It was not what he wanted, but he accepted the job offer
to provide for us. He hated it, and it did nothing to improve his disposition.
He came home tired, unhappy, and smelled of fumes. Discontent evolved
into a sense of hopelessness for both of us. We grew more unhappy, and
this drove a wedge into our relationship. We tried, talked about faith, and

took breaks from each other when needed, but there was no help in sight. Bodie's depression progressed, and I had no knowledge of how to help him.

He made efforts to adjust to our new environment. Bodie even cut his long hair to a more socially acceptable length. This was significant for him, more so than either of us expected. It was a great loss, and a form of surrender—of giving up. His hair had been a symbol of his masculinity, his strength, his power, and his Native American identity. Now it was gone.

We had moved back to Iowa because I was unhappy and now, he was unhappy. The life we once knew faded, and our marriage was crumbling. As the downward spiral continued, I felt helpless, but all I knew to do was to carry on. I continued to make homemade meals every day, kept a perfect house, had our baby girl dressed up every night when her daddy got home, and loved my husband fiercely. It was not enough. We had been married about two and a half years when things came to a head.

Our love struggled, and arguments increased. Our marriage was failing. We were young and there were so many things about life and marriage we didn't know. Communication was not on the agenda, and counseling didn't cross our minds. Neither of us had gone through counseling for the issues we grew up with. We were young, vulnerable, and flawed with no knowledge or awareness about what to do. My parents argued and struggled but they always went on without fail. I thought that was what you do.

Bodie didn't have a foundation for working through the situation we were in, and I believe his dark background had somehow set the stage for his future. We did the best we could with the one thing we were both sure of—how much we loved each other and our beautiful, precious baby girl. Still, despair took over, and lost hope won out.

We had reached the end of our road. The dark cloud once looming on the horizon increased in velocity and intensity. A deadly storm approached.

CHAPTER 7

TRAGEDY STRIKES WITH A FURY

Someone I loved once gave me a box full of darkness.
It took me years to understand that this too, was a gift.

— Mary Oliver

L ove, loss, and the unrelenting wrath of guilt would soon change my life forever. Even though Bodie and I hated conflict, as the friction in our marriage escalated, we fought. It was not unusual for him to leave in his van for a cooling-off period. When emotions calmed down, he would come home, usually in a couple of hours, and we would talk. I looked forward to his return when we would make up, usually under the covers. This behavior had become a familiar pattern.

In 1978, during a cold, harsh Iowa winter, the night was dark and freezing with ice on the roads. Although Bodie and I gave our marriage everything we had, it was not working. He was unhappy. His cooling-off breaks became more frequent. Arguments intensified and hope waned. One day our argument was the worst we'd ever had. In the heat of the moment, teeming with anger and frustration, I said, "I want a divorce," immediately regretting those words, but it was too late. Bodie left, mumbling under his breath, and slamming the door behind him.

A startling early morning knock on the door woke me. Our two dogs guarded me as I opened it. Two men in black suits stood outside. I was frightened. The dogs barked viciously. *Who were these men? Where was Bodie? Why wasn't he home yet?* It was out of character for him to stay gone this long. The men advised me they were from the coroner's office and showed me their badges. They asked if they could come indoors. I reluctantly agreed. The dogs hovered at my side as I sat on the couch. Something was terribly wrong. They sat across from me and leaned in with their hands on their knees as they told me my Bodie had died. His van veered off the highway into a concrete pillar and he died instantly, suffering no pain.

I immediately went numb, probably shock. I was unable to capture all they told me other than they said no other vehicles were involved and no alcohol or drugs were associated with the accident. *I needed them to leave.*

"Is there someone you can call, or we can call for you, someone who can come and be with you?" one of them asked.

I called Mom but couldn't reach her. In a daze, I called my parents' neighbors and told them my husband had died, and I couldn't get ahold of my mom. They went to my parents' house and woke them up. The coroners then knocked on my immediate neighbor's door and got her to sit with me until my parents got there, I was grateful for her presence. She held me, as I was numb, shaking, and unable to speak. By the time my parents arrived, a dark, turbulent time had begun in my life. It would be years before I would regain my footing.

The numbness stubbornly endured. People came. I couldn't talk. The pastor came. I couldn't talk. But I listened. Someone said I should be hospitalized for shock. Angel slept through that cold, dark night—the night my world collapsed. She was tucked safely in her crib with her "blankie," not knowing her Daddy, who loved her so much, was gone, forever.

As I sat on the bed in my room the following day with Mom, Dad, and the pastor, I was finally able to utter a few words. I didn't want to be hospitalized. I wanted—needed—to stay with my baby and the dogs.

Food arrived that day—lots of fabulous food—trays of it, bowls of it, pans of it. Although I was thankful for the thoughtfulness, I was unable to eat or sleep. Other people grazed. Eventually, my parents asked me if they could take Angel to their home to remove her from the chaos of the activity in the house and the trauma I was experiencing. I agreed. She would be better off there. They packed her bag and left me in the care of other people.

Angel stayed with them until after the services at which time I was able to care for her. I needed her—someone to hold on to. She was all that was left of us—Bodie and me. A sense of being unanchored tormented me—a chilling, frightening aloneness. A sense of guilt—that I had caused this—lurked in the recesses of my mind.

In the ensuing days, Mom was a rock and Dad was a steady influence. I was thankful for them especially when nighttime breakdowns terrorized me. Unanchored and free falling again, my world had collapsed around me. *Without Bodie at my side, how can I go on?*

The coroners delivered details of the horrendous, devastating news. A witness saw the car crash and Bodie's death was ruled *motor vehicular suicide*. What happened and why, only God knows. My mind was ravaged with questions that would remain unanswered. They swirled in my head as I mulled over *why's* and *what if's*. What happened that night? What was he thinking? Were the authorities correct? Were his actions some sort of self-fulfilling prophecy? The hopelessness of never knowing and the overwhelming trauma from what happened owned me. I was a mess. Left with a burden of guilt, but cognizant enough to be thankful Angel and I were not with him, I struggled to carry on.

As the numbness faded, I tried rationalization to make sense out of something nonsensical. Many people get into arguments and people get divorced, but they do not end their lives. Why didn't he have a foundation of coping strategies? Why didn't he sustain hope? No matter what I had gone through, a total loss of hope was never a consideration. Many people have had broken hearts. What drove Bodie's behavior? Years later, I would come to understand how Bodie may have been adversely affected by the circumstances of his life and the demons of his past. But I was never able to successfully rationalize what he did—if he did it.

As I pondered the why of Bodie's decision, I recalled the song, *Turn! Turn! Turn!* by the Byrds that he had told me he wanted played at his funeral. A song important to him, it delivered a profound message: "To everything there is a season." Why did he have a song for his funeral at such a young age, and why did he share it with me? *Couples must do that for funeral plans when they get married,* I thought, rationalizing his motive.

I recalled that day he told me his song choice for his funeral. We were young, and the thought distressed me. It struck me as odd, and I became concerned he had a song already picked out to have played at his funeral. As much as I tried—as a teenager with a zest for life—I couldn't think of a song for my funeral. I thought: *Sure hope I don't die because I don't have a song, other than "I Am Woman, Hear Me Roar," and that isn't appropriate.* After Bodie died, my mind took me back to that day and the profoundly prophetic significance of his words.

I had been unable to see the warning signs at that time in our lives and to recognize the depth of despair that swallowed him. There had been no suicide attempts or statements. There was no note. No known clinical depression. He loved his little Angel so much, and Bodie and I were joined at the hips, a Romeo and Juliet. *Was what happened meant to be?*

Going through his things, I ran across something Bodie wrote long ago, titled: "To Live Life, To Love One, and To Die." *Had he always had a preoccupation with death? Was it something that constantly lured him? Was I his last hope, the last straw in his life?* These questions and more would never be answered.

Bodie's casket was open at the funeral. The funeral director said Bodie looked good. *How can he look good? He's dead?* As it turned out, he didn't look good. *His appearance was anything but good.* One side of his face was affected by the crash—where he had turned his face before impact. The shock of seeing him was too much. With one look, I crumbled to the floor of the funeral home.

Days came and went. Many condolences were expressed, and a flurry of flowers arrived. Bodie's company felt awful for not having a life insurance policy and sent beautiful roses and a small check. My home looked like a florist shop as bouquets poured in. How does one comfort someone who just became a widow at nineteen with a nineteen-month-old daughter? The flowers were pretty, but a reminder of his death. All intentions were good, but I was inconsolable. Nothing mattered. I went to the Social

Security office with my mother and sobbed my eyes out the entire time. People stared at me. The loss was overwhelming. I cried all day, every day, everywhere.

My health deteriorated; I lost a lot of weight. The doctors put me on so many pills that I couldn't keep them straight. I laid them out on the counter every day and took them at will. My parents insisted I move out of the house and into an apartment closer to them. They helped me move.

Sad and lonely—damaged, in fact—I didn't talk much but cried, day after day. I didn't know how to move past that painful and hurtful time. I could not see the future and didn't have a circle of friends to support me. Crushing loneliness overtook me, and I was not coping well with day-to-day duties. I didn't know how to balance a checking account or what to do if the old car broke down. What do I do with his clothes? I didn't want to get rid of his clothes. I held them. They smelled of him. Then, someone took his clothes.

His family invaded my home and took things. They took his tools and left me with just a hammer. I do not recall giving permission. They helped themselves to whatever they wanted. In a daze, I was beyond the ability to help myself and became vulnerable to others taking advantage of me. And they did.

Bodie's prized possession, his Les Paul guitar, disappeared. I wanted it for Angel. Didn't they know that a husband's possessions go to the wife, and she decides what to do with them? They repeatedly tried to guilt me out of things. My mother took Bodie's treasured rifle out of the house to hide it in her attic to preserve it for Angel. It was one of the few possessions left of Bodie's and a gift from his grandfather. I was bullied and robbed blind. Without the fortitude to stand up for myself, I became a victim. A couple of Bodie's family members even blamed me for his death. One said, "I should have killed you." So, this is the kind of family Bodie grew up with. I was beginning to understand the root of some of his problems.

As if Bodie's death was not enough to almost kill me in and of itself, to be blamed for it was cruel and devastating. Tormented, I agonized over such thoughts and what I could have done to prevent it. Was it my fault? I was leaning in that direction, but I knew without a doubt that despite our difficulties, an intense and undeniable love between Bodie and I was still smoldering when he died. We were the love of each other's lives. To be made to feel responsible for the death of someone I loved so deeply was a horrendous thing to experience. Never, ever under any circumstances would I want my sweet Bodie and the father of our child dead. The aftermath was the most painful, dark, and worst time of my life. Guilt provoked by accusatory words from Bodie's family members followed me for years.

My grief was complicated. Left with a burden of guilt, intense layers of hurt, loss, and regret, I was exhausted, broken, lonely, dazed, and traumatized. A grief-stricken young widow with no foundation for enduring or finding my way through the fierce consequences of life, I suffered. I missed Bodie so much. My heart hurt, and the emotional pain was unbearable. I couldn't sleep at night. I lay in bed lamenting that he would never be by my side again. What can I do? How can I get through another day? Angel was the answer. He left me with a gift. Angel saved me. I held on tight to her—my reason to carry on with another day.

Bodie—my sweet Bodie—was my first love, and I his. But we couldn't live with each other, and we couldn't live without each other. We didn't make it; we couldn't make it. It was devastating. We still loved each other to the end and his little girl was his pride and joy. Questions with no answers filled my mind. Whatever the answers, the fact is that we had both been through a lot for such young people—things we were not equipped to handle. And we had no sense of the need to reach out for support. The dark cloud that hovered became the perfect storm that took him away.

The questions were never ending. They surfaced over and over throughout the years. Was Bodie's death from suicide? If the coroners were correct and it was, how could he hurt us and leave us so wounded? Why? Did he have a notion his action would set us free? Or was he too overtaken by his internal demons to even consider us? Was it a selfish act or an impulsive hasty decision that caused him to take his life? Was he blinded from hurt by our battered marriage?

I knew if Bodie had realized what this would do to us, he would not have done it. Was it a sacrifice of love or had he completed his purpose in life—*to live, to love one, and to die*? Had he come to set me free, give me a daughter, my sweet Angel, and put me on a path I was destined to walk? Questions. More questions. And no answers. The only thing I knew for certain was that, through death, Bodie had realized his desire to be a free bird. He always wanted to be free. And now he was.

I, on the other hand, lived in a kind of abyss. It tore me up when Angel didn't understand and called out for her daddy as she peered out the window, looking for him to come home from work—something she had done every day since she learned to walk. She and the dogs knew the sound of the van and had a sense of the time he would come home, always going to the window to wait for him. He never came home. I picked her up and held her. Our hearts were broken. We did things together as I endeavored to preoccupy her as much as possible. My dear mother was a saint in the aftermath of the crisis. However, despite everyone's best efforts, the road to my healing had to be traveled alone. Beyond a broken heart, somehow, I had to heal myself. Could I? Could I make it on my own without Bodie?

My husband's mother and stepfather moved back to Iowa. She had suffered a huge loss, and I hurt for her. However, she tried to take over, even worse than she previously did in Ohio. Bodie was her favorite son, and his daughter was a reminder of him. I felt smothered by her overreaching behavior, and even threatened in a sense. How far would she go to access her granddaughter? I couldn't risk the prospect of her interference. I had to get away from that threat. It was too real. So, I did what I always did to solve a problem. I bolted.

CHAPTER 8
A PATTERN OF FIX AND FAILS
CIRCLING THE DRAIN

My solution to problems established as a teen again tempted me. Back then, I ran away from home twice, and both times I failed on my own. Even my marriage was a fix, one that ultimately failed when Bodie died. Things had not gone well in Des Moines after his death. I lived next to people in my apartment who offered me drugs to console me. As druggies do, they stole from me, including a sentimental piece of jewelry. I had urges to run even before this incident, and this was the final nudge I needed to leave. I had a sister in Houston and that made it okay with Mom and Dad for me to take off for Texas. So, I bolted again to Texas.

Since my rebellious years as a teenager, I don't think my parents knew what to do with me. I was strong willed and a challenge to manage. They were tired and so was I, but they always believed in me, and they never wavered in that belief. I told them it was hard for me to stay in the same town where Bodie died. I needed to find my way and a new life for Angel and me. I assured them Angel and I would be fine. They seemed to understand that it was something I needed to do. Staid, midwestern people who rarely showed emotion, no doubt they were sad and worried as I headed off in search of a fresh start for myself and my little girl.

I was hopeful when I left Iowa. The U-Haul was packed. Angel and I said our good-byes and drove from Des Moines, Iowa, to Houston, Texas. On a quest to find myself and redeem my life, or so I thought, I was determined to make it there. *I will be free. Angel and I will have a fresh start.* But things often do not turn out so well when your plan is that you have no plan. I was a foolish, naive young girl running from the demons of my past.

I arrived in Houston optimistic and excited for a brighter future. I was eager for the opportunity to be close to my sister and looked forward to rebuilding our relationship after all the years since she left home. But she was in the midst of a demanding career, had a boyfriend, and lived quite a distance from me. I saw her only on rare occasions.

I wanted to love again. I wanted a new beginning. I couldn't help but think that Angel and I, two blondes, would be *a good catch*. I met a cute blond tennis player who I had a strong attraction to; however, with all my insecurities, I didn't feel I deserved him. *Surely if he knew everything about me, he would not want me. So*, I didn't pursue the relationship further.

As time passed, the high hopes I had for Angel and me in our new environment faded. I struggled and couldn't get my footing in Houston. There was an intrusive void in my life that I didn't know how to fill. For the first time, I was on my own, and I didn't manage that well. I made poor decisions. My life had been a mess, and now again it was a mess.

I returned my focus to my flute, the one thing that reminded me I was somebody and that I mattered. It was my light and my fire that always believed the best in me. I enrolled in flute lessons. If only I could play, everything would be okay. It wasn't, and although I tried to play, I couldn't, and feelings of failure and unworthiness shadowed me. I stopped going to lessons but held my flute close in my heart. Someday I would play again, just not today. That part of me was something that would never die.

Once I started dancing, I numbed myself with drugs and alcohol. Partying became a distraction—an anesthetic for the pain of trauma from molestation, teenage rebellion, a failed marriage, the death of my husband, and the accompanying guilt and loss. All that mess followed me from Iowa. Even the failure to realize my flute career haunted me.

My sister showed up unexpectedly at my apartment one day after I had started dancing at the club. I was dressed and ready for work. She looked at me and asked if I was going somewhere. I said I had a date. She just looked at me with eyes wide open as I smiled and nodded my head. I'm certain she suspected I was up to no good, but we had so little contact that we never discussed that awkward situation.

I had let down everyone I cared for. The emotional pain from all this was severe and unrelenting. It hurt so much. Alcohol and drugs kept me hanging on, but ultimately and predictably, they fostered disaster. Angel was with a babysitter for my "party times," and fortunately, I had a good babysitter. However, guilt tormented me because I was not the mom she needed and deserved. This piled on another layer of guilt. I was buried, and at death's door.

Angel deserved more. She deserved the best, and I couldn't give it to her. She had lost her dad, and *it was my fault.* Now I was letting her down. Festering guilt ate at me because of what I perceived as my role in my husband's death. *Had we not gotten into an argument or had I done this, or that, Angel might still have her daddy.* A vicious, unbearable cycle of pain and torment battered me. I hurt so bad.

Houston's party life provided a distraction for all those painful feelings. I was twenty years old, a foxy, alluring single woman, and it was party time in "party city." I met an Elvis Presley impersonator working at a club downtown. I abandoned my principles and let him move in with me for a brief time. I returned home one day to find him gone. He took his belongings as well as some of mine. I was "all shook up."

The downturn continued. I was having blackouts as my alcohol consumption increased. More guilt. And more drugs. A vicious cycle. I was mystified one morning when I awoke to discover my car banged up, and another time I woke up to discover it was gone. I didn't know where I had left it or how I got home the night before. Thank God I did get home somehow.

I had been circling the drain for some time, heading down a deep, dark hole. It became too hard to resist the promise that cocaine, speed, marijuana, alcohol, and a few other drugs in the mix would take away the pain. I was pummeled by a cyclone that shattered my life and almost left me dead. Each time I tried to gain my footing, I was knocked back down, even deeper into the depths of despair. Along this path, I received no counseling. I was lost.

I met a free-spirited, seventies hippie who offered me IV drugs. "Just try it," the glassy-eyed hippie lady said. "It doesn't hurt. Just stick the needle in your arm and the cocaine will take you higher." I guess everyone has a line they won't cross. This was mine. Amid my drug-induced haze, common sense kicked in, and I said no.

One day, as I drove down the highway at sixty-five mph with my daughter in the car, the hood flew up. As I navigated blindly off the highway, something inside of me broke. Pent up anger boiled to the surface. Every dreadful thing that happened to me happened because Bodie *abandoned me.* If he had not, I would have been a wife and mother living a normal life in Iowa. I missed him so much. But I was angry at him—and me.

Sitting in the car along the side of a freeway, I thought about how I needed Bodie. The anger exploded and I lost it. I bawled, I screamed, I ranted. I banged on the steering wheel. I needed Bodie. He would have made sure the hood of the car was shut. Bodie would have kicked the butt of all the people who abused me. He would have never allowed me to go off the deep end. He would have known what to do when the grease fire flared in the kitchen, when I got held up with a gun in a parking lot, and when giant Houston water bugs decided to have a party on the kitchen counter of the apartment. He would have helped take care of Angel if I needed to sleep. None of this mess of my life would have happened if he were here.

When I came to my senses, I peered into the back seat at my sweet, innocent little daughter. The worried and confused look on her face stormed into me. It was her and me now. I was all she had. *What am I doing? How can I sink so low? Can I save myself or is it too late? I must do it for her.*

I was whipped. Vulnerable, alone, scared, and out of control, I was one hot mess. But it took one more unfortunate incident to convince me to take action. A few days later, as I sat by myself on the side of the road at the midnight hour with two flat tires, I felt as though I was getting eaten alive in the dead of the night. Shock, numbness, tears, and guilt again turned into anger. My complex burden of grief continued to gnaw at me. I was going in and out of the grief cycle at any given minute and masking it with substance use when the pain became too much. Resentment welled up inside of me again—directed at Bodie and everything and everybody else. I was on the edge. Of what, I didn't know. I wanted desperately to get back on my feet and now this, and this, and this. A pathetic mess and feeling sorry for myself, even more guilt mounted as I faced the reality of my failures. *Had I reached rock bottom? Could I rally? Did I have it in me?*

CHAPTER 9

DIRTY AND MARRED, I FIGHT

A RECKONING AND A SOBER SURRENDER

Bodie's parents moved to Louisiana, which was not far from Houston. *Were they following me?* Every time I moved, they moved. They tried to influence me to move to Baton Rouge to be near them. I said, no. They didn't stop. Wanda, Bodie's mom, suggested Angel come stay with them for a while. I was hesitant because I had bolted because of her interference. *If I let Angel go for a visit, would they give her back to me?*

I knew I was in trouble and dancing on the edge of death's door. I didn't want Angel, who was three years old, at that time, around if my nonstop troubles increased, or something worse happened to me. It had been one thing after another. I had several close calls. I tried to rebound but could not manage to turn things around, and I could not be a good Mom. So, I succumbed to what I knew was best for Angel and took a risk. I sent her to be with Bodie's parents in Baton Rouge. The decision was an act of desperation, and it would have been incredibly selfish to do otherwise. This was to be only until I could get my life together and go retrieve her. I had to do what was best for her as hard as it was for me. I needed her, but she needed the stability and security Wanda could give her. I had to let her go.

I had minimal contact with my family while I lived in Houston. There were no cell phones in those days, so making phone calls was difficult. Mom wrote letters, but I rarely wrote back. I knew if I talked to her, she would know I was in a terrible situation. She instinctively knew everything.

The decision to send Angel to her grandparents tore me up. It was risky. *Were my in-laws interested in helping me or were they solely after what Wanda always wanted—Angel?* They never asked how I was or if they could help. Once Angel was gone, I missed her terribly. We were a team, and many times it was for her that I hung on each day. Now she was gone, and things got worse.

I had abandoned my daughter. *Let's just add another layer of torment to my messed-up life.* My decision haunted me, and the resulting inner turmoil and guilt ate away at my conscience. I rationalized my decision: *Bodie's mother is a connection for Angel to her father. Wanda can tell her stories—give her a piece of her dad and her Native American heritage. As years go on, the relationship can provide a cushion and comfort for Angel, another layer of family support. Even if I don't want a relationship with Wanda and her husband—or even like them after what their family did after Bodie's death—it is wrong for me to keep her from them. And, let's face it, I am desperate. I need help.*

I could only hope Angel wouldn't be exposed to "their dark side," the details Bodie described to me about his childhood. However, all indications were that Wanda's husband had mellowed and stopped drinking. Sadly, I concluded the risk of Angel remaining with me was greater than being with them. Also, if I denied Angel a relationship with them, how would she feel when she got older? Would she resent me for that? I began by giving them open visits. Angel got along well with them.

Although she was the catalyst that kept me sane, a beacon of light in my life and a reason to carry on, she was also a reason to change. So, I let her go "for a visit."

Wanda enrolled her in preschool. Angel stayed with them for about three months in total, after which my overwhelming guilt about not being the kind of mother I wanted to be compelled me to move to Baton Rouge. That was not the only reason, though. When Angel was gone, I had no responsibilities, and my partying escalated. The nightmare I experienced in Houston, which caused me to fear for my life, and my determination to crawl out of the pit of hell I had fallen into were also driving forces. Baton Rouge was calling. Wanda encouraged me to come. I wanted to trust her, but I feared she might not return Angel if I didn't move there and claim her. So, off I went to Louisiana to get my daughter and find a new beginning. This time I was running to something, more than from something.

I packed a U-Haul once again, my puppy and me, and drove to Baton Rouge. The geographical shift was medicine for both Angel and me. It offered a fresh start. *I will stop drinking, get a respectable job, and straighten out my life.* Despite all my troubles, I did have a burning drive and an underlying level of strength and spirit that spurred me to keep trying for a better life. I stumbled and fell. I got dirty and marred. But never did I concede defeat. Unlike my sweet Bodie, I fought for my life and my daughter, even when scraping bottom. Angel may see me on the floor after losing a battle, but she will never see me lose the war. I will not ever abandon her. *I won't give up. I won't surrender*—or so I thought. Little did I know that surrender was the medicine I needed to overcome my demons and save Angel's mother.

I leased a duplex, went, and got Angel, brought her home, and landed
a job working for the State of Louisiana. That boosted my confidence.
I purchased proper work clothes, a huge shift from my party wardrobe.
At first, they seemed excessively dowdy. I was shocked at how different
clothing choices made me feel, and that discrepancy made me realize how
far off track I had gone. The new work wardrobe became a symbol of my
recovery, but I had this gnawing feeling that I was faking something. *That's
okay. I'll fake it until I make it.* Or so I thought.

I started going to church and found a new boyfriend, a strait-laced kind of
guy, a church boy. He once came to my home with two bouquets of long
stem red roses, one for me and one for Angel. That act meant more than I
could say. Donny was a good guy. If only he knew....

I sang in the choir at church, smiling out at Donny as he sat in the audience,
and went home and drank strong liquor. I soothed my misery by increasing
the Kahlua crème in morning coffee. I progressed to vodka later in the day
and switched to scotch in the evenings. I hid my habit well, but the guiltier
I felt, the more I drank. The difference this time was that I only drank at
home, and I drank alone. I was done with being on the side of the road
at night with two flat tires and the other atrocities that happened when I
drank outside the home.

Crazy things happen when alcohol takes over one's life. I had tried hard to
beat my addictions by shear willpower. I was able to easily give up drugs
and pills, except for occasional marijuana, but alcohol owned me. I took
my pocket Bible to work every day to read on breaks, thinking that reading
the Psalms would comfort me and help me change. But that didn't work.
Alcohol had a talon grip on me, and it was tightening.

My double life led to further devastation. One day, I drove as far as I could go with no destination in mind. Angel was at her grandma's. I had no idea where I was going. *Just drive.* I came to a waterfront and pulled in. Irrational thoughts swirled in my mind. I wanted to drive into the water. I needed to stop the madness. I had tried, and tried, and tried. And I failed. It was one thing after another. Tired, weathered, and worn, I fell asleep in the car.

I woke up to rays of sun shining on me, warming my body. Something clicked and I had a *come to Jesus* experience. I expressed my anger with fury. I pounded the steering wheel as I raged. *Damn it. Bodie could do it. He could end his misery. I can't.* I couldn't do it, thinking of my sweet Angel, I couldn't do it. I was mad at Bodie and God. I had given up on understanding Bodie, but I had still searched for God. And He was not there. *Why did you take Bodie from me and Angel? Why do I have to go through hit after hit, after hit? If Jesus died so I might live, I wasn't doing a particularly good job of it. Maybe I can't make it. But I must.* Realizing I got no answers to my questions that day and craving a drink, I took my sad, sorry ass home.

I was not well—mentally, emotionally, or physically. My drinking continued and increased in volume. *Now I am stuck with my in-laws, who have their noses in my business and are telling me what to do. I hate my job, and I hate my stupid clothes.*" I took on another layer of guilt over lying about the heavy drinking while singing in the choir. In a vicious cycle, I drowned my sorrows in alcohol. *I had become a pathetic victim, a poor persecuted soul.*

Angel was happy and easily entertained herself with her toys. She played house, cooked in her play kitchen, and took care of her dolls. Other than my morning Kahlua and coffee, most of my drinking went on after she went to sleep in the evenings. Life was dark and bleak, I was barely hanging on. My move to Baton Rouge increased the drinking and the cycle of despair. I worried about myself but concluded that no one cared about me. I uttered a simple prayer: *God, if you are real, please help me.* I was angry at Him, whoever He was. I didn't like Him, and I knew for sure He didn't like me. I was so-o-o done. *F - - - it! F - - - you, too, God!*

Little did I know, things were about to change. Desperate times called for desperate measures. An intervention was in the works. I had fooled no one. It was a Sunday afternoon in Baton Rouge. My mother-in-law, the church pastor, and Donny showed up at my home. They directly and succinctly took me to task, shortly after which the phone rang. It was my mother. She asked me to please return to Iowa. How embarrassing. My church boyfriend, pastor, and Wanda in my home for an intervention and Mom on the phone. *How clever were they. They had conspired to confront me. And I thought no one knew and no one cared.* I was shocked and confused.

Mom had arranged for a hospital in Des Moines to help me. She would take care of Angel for six weeks while I went. *Surely, I don't have an alcohol problem. I have a lot of other problems, but who wouldn't if they experienced all I had endured.* I looked at the faces staring at me and realized how exhausted I was, weary from years of fighting battles. I needed rest. I loved my mother and trusted her with Angel. I was astounded and relieved that Wanda was willing to let her go to my mom. These people were all here for me. I was wrong—so wrong. I was not in this all alone. They cared about me. I surrendered.

Although my mind was foggy at the time, I will never forget the day I entered rehab in February 1980. Through the haze, I recognized that I needed help even though my self-awareness was stymied. But I didn't know why. I just knew I was so very tired and broken. And I loved my mother. I wanted my mommy. I would climb back into the womb if I could and start over with a new life.

Mom delivered me to rehab. I asked the lady signing me in what I was there for. She said for alcohol treatment. I told her I might have other problems, but alcohol was not one of them. She assured me, in a calming voice, "This was a good place to start, and if there are other problems, we can also help you with them."

I advised her that I had *a whole lot of problems*, and if she had my life, she would have problems, too. I looked at Mom, my sweet Mom, and noted the pain in her face. I would do anything for my mom. And so, it was. I surrendered.

I was admitted into alcohol treatment in the State of Iowa at the age of twenty-one. I was such a challenge initially that the treatment staff requested an extension beyond the thirty-day inpatient treatment standard. They were confident their program would work, but it would take time. I had to work through significant grief and guilt issues from numerous traumas that had stolen my innocence, my adolescence, and my young adult years.

The treatment was tough, ruthless, and brutal. I had to sit around and tell a room full of people how I had wronged others who had wronged me. *How could this be? This takes the cake.* I soon learned that many of the things I had been through were called *unmanageables*. They said I had numerous *unmanageables*, but I was not allowed to feel sorry for myself. I was told that self-pity was like "putting a noose around your neck." That was a fresh perspective, but one hard to swallow. Of all things, hadn't I been through enough and now, they say I am not permitted to feel sorry for myself? *OMG. That is mind boggling....*

I was required to write a list of everything I had done to harm others. Then I had to sit in a large room filled with a circle of people and read it aloud. There weren't enough items on my list. So, I was instructed to write more and try again the next day. "Dig deeper," the counselor said.

"Are you kidding me?" I responded. It was a gut punch to read aloud how I had hurt my mother, my daughter, myself, and others. Especially, I had endangered my daughter's life by driving under the influence. Day after day after day, I humbled myself by announcing an extensive list of my failings until the counselors were satisfied. It was raw, as raw as it gets, but it was the necessary first step to beginning the wretched climb out of the pit I was in—a vital step to regaining my life. The experience was so gut wrenching that, to this day, I have never had another drink of alcohol.

The treatment was a time of reckoning, a turning point in my life. The brain fog from alcohol and drugs lifted. I took hold of "the AA program," just as counselors began to question whether I could. The layers of trauma had deeply affected me, and it took longer than normal to uncover it all and purge the demons. I took to the program and ran with it. In just shy of six weeks, I graduated. I felt like a new person at the ceremony. My counselor stood and shared how proud and confident she was of me and the road ahead. Ms. AA I would be. I would do everything by the "big book," and I set out to do all I was told I needed to do. I learned that alcoholism was an illness like having diabetes. There were ongoing actions I had to do to maintain my sobriety. This made sense, something I could grasp and do. Until....

I returned to Baton Rouge after completing treatment with some of my guy friends from the program to help me move back to Des Moines to be near my family. Angel stayed with Mom during my treatment and move. During the move, one of the guys pulled out a line of cocaine. I told him, "No. We aren't supposed to do that," but he insisted that one time wouldn't hurt. I knew better, but I was feeling vulnerable around my new friends who were there to help me move. Their rationalization of the treatment program clashed with what I had learned, nevertheless, I succumbed to the temptation, after which I felt horrible.

I remembered what the counselor said, "Only five percent of the people who go through treatment make it. The other ninety-five would result in death, insanity, or incarceration." That scared me. I had a daughter who needed me and a family who loved me. I was not an idiot. I was going to be in that five percent if it took everything in me. The unfortunate relapse derailed me, but it only happened one time. I was disappointed in myself as my sobriety date moved to April 15 after the incident. I have now been free of both alcohol and drugs for forty-four years.

I journeyed home to Iowa from Baton Rouge. I had lost the privilege to drink for the remainder of my life. Drugs and opiates were off the agenda as well.

I had whipped my demons, thrashed them like the evil fiends they were. I was woman, hear me roar. I was a daughter devoted to the woman who birthed me. I was a mom, defending her cub. And I was finally okay.

Was I really an alcoholic or was it trauma and sexual abuse that drove me to drinking? Today, I don't feel tempted to drink. Occasionally, I think about what it would be like to have a drink of wine or champagne, but the thought diminishes quickly as I associate alcohol with my dark valley of hell. I have reserved my 90th and 100th birthday for a sip of champagne and have instructed my daughter and family to get the stretcher ready for my toast. We laugh; however, they keep their opinions to themselves concerning the remote possibility I will realize my wild milestone birthday plans.

Angel was my everything, my reason to get back up when life knocked me down, my reason to change, to fight, and the reason I got clean and sober. As I look back on that unstable time, I realize how fortunate I am to be alive. Additionally, I had no confrontations with the police or social services with my drinking and drug use, although I deserved it at times. I am thankful my precarious walk "in the valley" was short lived. It was awful and hard on me, as well as on Angel and my mother. After all that, I vowed to pursue a life of service to others. And I did.

I demonstrated tenacity and embraced a transformation once I mastered a "set of rules" to live by and developed a better understanding of myself and what happened to me. I dug deep when in treatment as a traumatized young, grief-stricken widow and mother. The key to overcoming was personal accountability—I was responsible for cleaning my side of the street no matter what others had done to me. I had offended and wronged others, and I learned to hold myself accountable for those mistakes. I was required to "make amends" and apologize to everyone I had wronged. It was one of the hardest things I've ever done, but I did it. From then on out, I was determined to be Ms. AA and follow my "instructions for life."

After treatment, I embraced others with respect and dignity while learning to love them as well as myself. I forgave them and began the process of forgiving myself. I purged my soul. We are all flawed. We all make mistakes. We are all human. I attended AA meetings and got a sponsor.

I met many amazing people who loved unconditionally no matter who you were or what you had done. This program was a gift. It reflects how peaceful society could be in a perfect world, rich with unconditional love, acceptance, respect, and self-responsibility.

I studied the twelve steps to recovery and explored the concept of a higher power as the path to understanding spiritualism. I sought a nonjudgmental attitude toward all humanity. I was not sure about the "God thing" after all I had suffered. I didn't have all the answers and didn't spend much time contemplating the mysteries of spiritual conventions. I was simply grateful to be alive and preoccupied with living. I was just a girl from Madison County, Iowa, battered, but no longer broken. I was clean and sober. The healing, though, was in the early stages.

CHAPTER 10

IS THIS HEAVEN? NO. IT'S IOWA

NOT A GOOD FIT? BOLT

Nestled in the center of the midwestern heartland, an area known as the world's breadbasket, Iowa rates only second to California in agricultural production. Ninety percent is rich black, silky soil and is dedicated to growing corn, soybeans, and pork, as its primary products. A land of farms, its most populous city, Des Moines, has a population of around 200,000. Harsh winters are offset by three other seasons that produce prolific fields that help feed the world. Someone said, "Is this Heaven? No. It's Iowa." That may be a bit of an overstatement. Culturally, some of the state's greatest attributes also proffer unfortunate downsides. Someone said, "Iowa is a wonderful place to grow up, if you live your whole life there. If you leave, brace yourself. You may be ill prepared for the world outside."

Iowa was populated mostly by northern European immigrants who traversed through Pennsylvania, Ohio, and Illinois during this country's early western migration. Steeped in that old world culture, its population emerged into what has been called a White, Anglo-Saxon, Protestant (WASP) mentality wherein rigid religious and conservative social values and cultural norms were diligently enforced. Over the years those influences have been tempered, but I grew up in Iowa's highly structured, right, and proper world.

Iowa is now known for Hawkeye football, one of the largest state fairs in the country, its notoriously unique and quirky political caucuses, and a top-of-the-line education system, which delivers one of the highest literacy and graduation rates in the nation. Hollywood's interest in Iowa is reflected in a book and a 1995 film, *The Bridges of Madison County*. Many visitors flock to Winterset to see the famous bridge in the movie, the one so familiar to me as a child.

For me, Iowa involved growing up in a world filled with traditions, conservative values, and simplicity that protected me in many ways from the "world outside." I was burdened with feelings of shame and guilt when I left Iowa. I was also incredibly naive and unprepared for the circumstances I would face. The cultural differences between Des Moines and Houston at that time cannot be overstated. As a result, I took some hard licks. However, I was calling the shots, and, at the end of the day, I was accountable for my actions. I have no one to blame but myself for my poor judgment—not my family, not my husband's suicide, and not Iowa.

I moved back to Iowa in 1980, after my brief stint in Louisiana, and secured a duplex for Angel and me. Life took on a new direction as I adjusted to clean and sober living. Our home had a yard for Angel's swing set and a sand box. She quickly made friends in the neighborhood. A large area of untended fertile soil backed up to the property. I inquired about the empty field and after getting approval, had it plowed. I had a dream—a beautiful, lush garden full of melons and vegetables of every kind. I went to work and designed and cultivated a large garden. I loved digging in the rich, black Iowa dirt and watching things grow. Doing so healed my soul and nurtured my recovery. I tended the garden daily as I had watched both my parents and grandparents do.

Not one to do things half-way, I went all out and planted all types of edibles. I enjoyed picking fresh lettuce, cabbage, radishes, cucumbers, tomatoes, and green beans. I dug up potatoes and pulled up carrots and onions. How I loved harvesting sweet, ripe strawberries, watermelons, and cantaloupes. BLT sandwiches, garden salads, and freshly husked sweet corn were regular meals for Angel and me. An abundance of fresh garden produce was shared with family, friends, and neighbors.

It was a season of hope, healing, and resiliency—a hope that someday I would be able to provide Angel with all she deserved and all I wanted for her. I taught Angel the basics for playing the piano, and she eventually went on to take piano and voice lessons. She excelled in everything she did. She blossomed.

I wished she didn't have a mom who had to walk the journey that was set before me. I had more healing to do on a long road to recovery. I wanted her to have a perfect family, two parents, siblings, a white picket fence, and a dog. I tried to focus on reality—what I might be able to give. Because I stumbled and fell in the past and got back up, over, and over, perhaps I could teach her resilience? Those early experiences were rocky, bumpy, and turbulent. I hoped that someday, she would understand and forgive me for my flawed ways. Until all my dreams for her could come true, I held her tight.

Although I had given up alcohol and drugs, I still smoked a pack of cigarettes a day. I had smoked since I was fifteen years old. Chronic episodes of bronchitis began to affect my health. It progressively worsened, and I couldn't catch my breath. So, I quit—cold turkey. I made up my mind to quit, and I did. I had two drags in the days after that decision, and it was so nasty, I never again smoked. Another vice eliminated—more progress on my healing journey.

My in-laws soon decided they too wanted to move back to Iowa after I left Baton Rouge. I wasn't surprised. But what I didn't know was that Wanda had a secret. *Was I correct in being concerned when I sent Angel to live with her?* I soon learned that Wanda's husband, Bob, was a practicing alcoholic. I had let Angel go to their home for three months with the understanding he wasn't drinking. Wanda insisted he didn't drink until Angel had gone to sleep; however, her state of denial explained why he wasn't present at my intervention. Why had she not intervened with him? Again, Wanda became a thorn in my side. And I blamed her for taking up with a man who contributed to Bodie's issues. His childhood was marred by her defense of her husband, and we paid a huge price for that.

I soon learned the answer to this quandary as I realized that solving this problem was up to me. Bob asked me one day how I got sober, and I became an unofficial mentor and sponsor for him. This was not something I signed up for. It happened organically. Although I had a lot of weight on my shoulders, I took it on. Everything I did in recovery, he did. He followed me. Somedays the weight was too much for Bob. "How did you do it, Joan?" he asked. I revealed my experiences, my secrets. As a recovering alcoholic, my life was an open book.

My healing didn't stop there. I started going to church, and guess who else started going to church. It became increasingly evident that Wanda and Bob's daily life revolved around Angel and me. They were always in my business, and for Wanda I could never do anything right. *God, that prayer*

I prayed to help me kick alcohol, can you help me again? Please get my in - laws occupied with something, anything! I need to focus on my own healing.

Time passed and healing led me down a new path—and not a good one. I developed an eating disorder. Oh, yes, another burden to bear. *Who am I? Job?* I was apparently destined to run a gamut of disorders. This one involved a preoccupation with weight, food restriction, deprivation, and calories. With a starting weight of 125 pounds, I got down to 105 on my five feet five-and-a-half-foot frame. This eating disorder ran for the span of several years. I soon discovered this didn't work well for me. I was getting unwanted attention from men, even getting some "booty calls." I needed to heal, and this was not helping. I did date and became involved with someone. Dusty wrote poetry about me, as sweet Bodie had done, which endeared me to him. But when he moved in and immediately quit his job, I kicked him out. Although the love between Dusty and me was intense, I didn't take him to raise. I could not be anyone's mama except Angel's—and, oh God, evidently my step father-in-law, Bob.

My eating disorder then swung in the other direction—from anorexia to compulsive overeating. *Why can't I just do something normal?* I gained around thirty pounds from my normal weight. I had no control over food. Binging, polishing off a half gallon of ice cream in one sitting, and eventually becoming addicted to laxatives took over my life. I was out of control once again and eating emotionally. Guilt overwhelmed me one morning after a binge. I was miserable and didn't know what to do, but I knew I needed to do something. In desperation, I joined Overeaters Anonymous. I began to work the program like I did for alcohol and drug use; however, doing so was more difficult because you can't just cut out eating.

I learned that a deeper issue drove my eating disorders. Some conditions are common for sexual abuse victims. Gaining weight is something sexually abused women unconsciously do to avoid sexual attention. Much of what I went through—from alcohol and drugs, running away, sexual acting out, and dancing—were common behaviors for sexual abuse victims. And I, being the determined diligent woman I am, tried them all. Many women never receive treatment and end up in prostitution and with severe drug addictions, which hampers any chance of recovery. Thankfully, I dodged those bullets. I was grateful for my family's intervention and the program I was given, which brought redemption and helped me crawl out of the pit I was in with alcohol. It brought me to focus on living my life one day at a time. And now, I applied those processes to this new eating disorder, one pound at a time.

Because of Bodie's death, I received Social Security to help raise Angel. But I was ambitious and wanted to work, to earn a living and provide for her all she deserved. I valued my independence and didn't want to rely on anyone else to provide for us. So, I decided to get an education. I began college classes at the Area Community College in Ankeny, Iowa, and completed an Associate Degree in Human Services with a specialty in Chemical Dependency Counseling. I then earned a license in the State of Iowa as a Substance Abuse Counselor. I went to school part-time so I could stay home to raise Angel and enjoy her many activities.

I transferred my credits to Drake University where, as a scholarship award winner with all tuition paid, I completed a Bachelor of Science Degree in Education and obtained a teaching license. I graduated Cum Laude and with Departmental honors in May 1986. I was on the Honor Roll, and the President and Dean's List. I took flute lessons, practiced, and played my flute in the Drake University Symphony. Drake was Dad's alma mater, and I made him proud the day I graduated with my younger sister—a grand occasion for our parents, family, and grandparents. It was a special day.

At this time, I was still very much in the healing stage from sexual abuse. I was overweight for my size, and, although throughout the years my long, blonde hair had been my pride and joy, I hacked it off into a mop-top style to assure I was not attractive and to create a protective barrier that thwarted advances from men. However, that didn't work. No matter what I did, those Iowa men were a determined bunch, and they were still after me.

I met a man at a church group, a widower, Bruce, whom I dated. I was skeptical of institutional religion and had begun to appreciate the genuine sincerity and goodness of the teachings of Bill Wilson and Dr. Bob Smith, founding members of Alcoholics Anonymous. But I was raised in the Presbyterian church and wanted to raise my daughter there. So, I "warmed the pews." Bruce, a well-to-do Iowa farmer, an usher in the church, and a respected member of the community, didn't care that I was overweight and had chopped - off hair. He had lost his wife to cancer. He appeared to be someone who would make me happy, and we became engaged. I had taken a vow of celibacy and that didn't seem to bother him. His mother was a big part of his life. She made such food as fried chicken and mashed potatoes for the farm hands' noon meal. She did everything she could to help me adjust, even teaching me how to make horseradish from a root in the ground. I worked hard to fit the role of a farmer's wife.

The date was set, the wedding cake was ordered, and a few gifts had arrived. However, a restlessness haunted me, and doubts could not be denied. So, we sought pre-marital counseling and eventually decided to take a pre-honeymoon trip to see if a getaway would help strengthen and solidify our relationship. We booked a trip to Egypt and Israel. It was on this trip that I learned that traveling together is a good litmus test for the viability of a relationship.

It was 1986, and I was twenty-eight years old. Our parents bid us goodbye, and we boarded a plane for Egypt. The trip was bittersweet. I suffered extreme jet lag and had not brought anything to help me sleep. The strange environment distressed me. In Cairo, men stared at my blonde hair. Extreme poverty, dirt, and the sounds of gunfire welcomed us. A couple of nights passed, and I had yet to sleep. By the third day, I was irritable and unsettled. Then, something inside of me broke, and I gave my beautiful one carat engagement ring back to my fiancé and said, "We are getting out of bondage." He was not amused. Then it sunk in, *what if he leaves me in Egypt by myself? Maybe I want that ring back.*

I recognized why I had decided to get married. I was trying to do right by my daughter and my parents by doing something my family wanted and fulfilling a role society, and others expected of me. But I was not a country girl. Something was missing. I had deep feelings for Bruce, but I was not in love with him. I needed time to explore my doubts without the wedding talk and plans. With the date only three weeks away, serious concerns plagued me. I thought getting away on this trip would bring clarity to my concerns, and it did. The marriage would be a mistake. It wasn't right for either of us. Trying to do what was right, I had messed up—another fix and fail.

I would only hurt Bruce if I married him. He was a sweet, honorable, and steady man, but the spark was not there. I knew what I had to do, and it wasn't going to be easy. I had to be honest about my feelings, and there was no way to do that without hurting him.

As Bruce put the ring in his pocket, I was so sad for him. We awkwardly continued the tour but didn't talk to each other much. People on the tour bus observed that something was wrong. I tried to engage him. I expected him to get angry, but he didn't. He was quiet. The relationship went cold for a few days but soon transitioned into a conversational mode as we found a way to enjoy the sights for the remainder of the trip.

I had worked diligently to preserve myself for marriage and now there would not be one. *Awkward. Good thing there were two twin beds at the hotels.* We continued the journey together, visiting historical sights and ancient civilizations. We rode camels, saw King Tuts tomb and museum, ate amazing fish, and climbed inside pyramids. Inside the dark, small staircase in the pyramids, someone on the opposite side reached over and grabbed my crotch. *Geez,* I thought to myself, but once again, after wanting to climb over the rail and give him a piece of my mind, I kept it to myself and carried on.

Feeling like I was in a daze from lack of sleep for a week, I climbed aboard the train we took to Tiberius. We eventually arrived in Tel Aviv, Israel, and I was able to sleep for the first time after much deprivation. Our journey then took us to Bethlehem and the Holy City of Jerusalem. The sights were breathtaking and memorable. The experience was like stepping into another world. We visited the Wailing Wall and the believed place of Jesus' crucifixion, ate fish at the Sea of Galilee, floated in the Dead Sea, and went to Mount Olives. Masada was a dark place—a site where in 73-74 B.C. up to 960 Jewish men, women and children took their own lives rather than fall into the hands of the Roman army.

It was the trip of a lifetime, yet bittersweet since I broke off the engagement. We journeyed home. I told my parents we called the wedding off, and my father said, "You will end up in a poor one-bedroom apartment." I knew I had hurt him, that he only wanted me to be taken care of, but the marriage was doomed. As one friend said, "The relationship was like putting a turtle and a racehorse on the same track together."

My fiancé, one of the nicest men I have ever known, paid off the china on our bridal registry after we arrived back home, and he paid for much-needed repairs to my car. Who does that? Bruce. He deserved the best, someone who would be a good farmer's wife. That person was not me. I was a city girl. He needed and deserved someone who loved to cook fried chicken and mashed potatoes for his hired hands and to help him with his bountiful, thriving farm full of Iowa corn and soybeans. What he needed was not me, although I very much wanted it to be. His world was not mine and trying to make it so would have been a mistake. We never spoke again after saying our final goodbyes.

I was completing an internship at an elementary school for my college degree requirements at that time and Angel was in school and involved in various activities. In the matter of a few short months, I had new neighbors. Guess who? Yes, my in-laws moved to the street behind me. I was now agitated. *No wonder my husband had problems.* I was trying graciously to facilitate a relationship between them and my daughter; however, it became more difficult by the day, and an uncomfortable restlessness churned inside of me. I became aware that, although well intended, their issues had damaged Bodie in his developing years, and he carried those scars into our marriage. I was torn between their intention to be devoted grandparents and the need to protect Angel from what her father experienced. They were too close. Everywhere I went, they went. I was eventually forced to cut ties.

Bob and Wanda were now active in a church. Bob chose a different route of recovery than I did. He abandoned AA and counseling and immersed himself in the church. Although I believe many people are helped that way, my personal belief stayed with the premise of a foundation of professional counseling by experts in the field. People trained in addiction can facilitate healthy new patterns of thoughts, actions, and behaviors. This would include managing anger, healthy relationships, boundaries, communication, and stress. The program taught me the importance of striving for balance in all elements of my life, which always brought me back to center. Bob and I would soon be parting ways. I knew he would be all right without me. He got a call offering him a job in ministry at the Salvation Army, and he accepted, going on to be a captain. I was thankful for something to distract him.

Angel was twelve years old. I wanted time with her and to raise her myself without the constant stress from interference and criticism from Bodie's family, who insinuated I was incompetent. And I never quite got over his family's treatment of me and a comment to me after the funeral that a family member wished they had killed me. All that on top of breaking my engagement troubled me. Angel was at the forefront of my mind as I pondered my situation. I wanted to give her my full attention and have her be my top priority. She had lost her father and had no siblings. I was determined to devote my life to her.

I needed to leave Iowa for what I hoped would be the last time. I was a woman who had been severely tested—one who had passed and one who was centered and grounded. I was not on the run, but rather, in pursuit of a bright future for my child and myself—a future we both deserved. I had earned a blazing, rousing rally, and I would, by God, make it happen in

Tulsa, Oklahoma. On a quest to discover my place in the world and what I was born to do, I bolted.

Part II

THE RALLY

CHAPTER 11

STAKING OUT GROUND

FINDING MY WAY AND MY NICHE

A traumatic past has a way of steeling a person for the role they were born to play. I didn't realize it then, but when I bolted in 1986 to Tulsa, I was on the cusp of a significant shift that would change the trajectory of my life. As a recent college graduate pushing thirty years of age, I had worked hard at redeeming myself after tumultuous teenage years as well as the self-induced traumas of my twenties when I struggled to heal from the burden of Bodie's death. I was ready for a second chance at life and determined to make it productive and meaningful.

I had disappointed my parents again by breaking off my engagement to Bruce who they believed offered me the stability that would give them peace and me security. But at this point, as I packed the U-Haul once again and headed south, I was in pursuit of a major comeback orchestrated on my terms. With the history of sexual abuse, my husband's death, and now, a broken engagement, I considered becoming a nun. Seriously. I was not up for more drama or the "romantic love thing." Those things had not worked out well for me. I was determined to behave myself and act in a manner to which I was not accustomed.

Not being Catholic, the closest thing to being a nun I could find
was at Oral Roberts University in Tulsa. The campus was impressive
with incredible architecture—large buildings adorned with sparkling gold
embellishments. The institution sent missionaries out into the world and
required celibacy and a healthy lifestyle. *That's it, I will go to seminary.*
So, off Angel and I went—south to Oklahoma. We were on our own and
determined to independently make our way in the world. *That would
make my parents proud.*

It was August when I arrived in Tulsa where I had been accepted into
ORU's Master of Divinity program in the School of Theology. The
Oklahoma temperatures were hot enough to fry bacon and eggs on the
pavement. I didn't know anyone, but the aloneness gave me a keen sense
of independence that felt good. Dripping with sweat, I moved us into the
Oral Roberts University apartments, took a vow of celibacy, and enrolled
Angel in school.

I studied hard, learned Hebrew, gave a sermon in front of a congregation
at an old country church, wrote my own funeral service, played flute in a
worship team, and was accepted to teach English as a second language in
China. My daughter and I studied the Mandarin language and prepared to
chart our course. However, my assignment was changed at the last minute
from Changchun, China, to another location with less than desirable
conditions and accommodations. I could risk everything, but I could not
make such a decision for Angel. So, I declined the position and decided
to write letters to Israel with an inquiry on being a missionary there. I
was turned down because of my daughter's age with recommendations
to do local missions in Tulsa. Not sure what I wanted to do, I continued
with my studies in religion and ideology. I loved to learn and had taken
a class on world religions while enrolled at Drake. Religion intrigued me;

however, the Southern religion differed from the conservative foundation I experienced in Iowa. My studies at ORU adhered to a rigid religious tone that conflicted with the spirituality and balance in life I sought. Still, I carried on with the University's program.

Students were required to serve, and I chose an assignment at the City of Faith—a three-tower hospital that served as a place of research and medical care with a Christian foundation associated with Oral Roberts ministry. I was placed as a prayer partner at the emergency room facility. Finally, everything was fine. I was grounded, dutiful, and reformed—until my eyes landed on one of the most gorgeous men I had ever seen.

I was trying to be good. I had worked to create a dowdy appearance unattractive to men. My hair was still mop-top, helmet-head short, and I was overweight. Also, as a student in seminary school, I had taken a vow of celibacy. I was devoted to praying with patients in the emergency room, as assigned, and minding my own business when, after laying eyes on this handsome man, I realized I wasn't dead yet.

Out of nowhere, I came face to face with Boaz, a dark-haired, award-winning body builder who was a Jewish doctor—of all things. *Oh No! A young Jewish body-building doctor? Be still my heart.* I had tried so hard to be good, and now this. *You've got to be kidding. I am in so much trouble! Run fast!* I couldn't. I was on duty. I had managed to thwart three other persistent pursuers at ORU, but *that was then, and this was now.* I caved.

I soon discovered what a good kisser my young hot Boaz was. *Good thing he is not my doctor. But maybe we could play doctor. Maybe I was suddenly healed of my trauma. Maybe this was meant to be, and he was the reason I came to ORU.* No doubt, he was special. He was intelligent, accomplished, sophisticated, and mysterious. What was he doing working in a Christian hospital as a Jewish man? He explained that the City of Faith had an excellent program on brain research, which was an integral part of his field of study. He didn't mind that it was a Christian hospital.

Boaz and I began seeing each other. He was doing his residency at the time, studying brain trauma and rehabilitation. I had an intense attraction to him, but our time together was cut short when his residency took him to another state. Evidently, he was not a gift from God after all. Like a bird that lands and then flies away, he was gone.

Weeks, months, and years, and still no word from him, leaving a hurtful imprint on my heart. I would see him only in my dreams and in the few photos that remained. Love flirted with me, and then it vanished. Although this hurt, and I was sad, I let go of him easily. The end was, as it turned out, a good thing. The experience changed me. I doubled down on my studies and returned to focusing on my appearance. I lost the extra weight, grew out my hair and reconsidered my wardrobe. Although this romance didn't endure long enough to mature into love, it teased me with the possibility of love, and I opened myself up to the prospect of finding it again.

Finances caught my attention because school loans and a loan from my parents had increased to an uncomfortable level. I became concerned about my ability to pay them off in a timely manner. So, in the middle of a sixty-hour program at ORU, I quit, blaming this impetuous act on divine intervention. The *spirit of debt* had taken hold, and it was time to go to work.

Another phase in my journey through life took hold. It was time to achieve independence. We moved out of ORU housing and into the community where I found part-time work as a behavioral weight loss counselor for Nutri System.

My daughter was approaching her teenage years, and we were close, although I knew this journey was not easy for her. I continued to hope she would see strength, hope, humanity, and resiliency in my choices. She was my joy. I reveled in everything she did. When I turned thirty, she planned and organized a surprise birthday party for me. Her love and joy touched me deeply, and I was proud of her initiative, competence, and devotion. With this special event, I realized how loved I was and how many friends I had.

The move to Tulsa opened new doors and opportunities, introducing me to many outstanding people. I played my flute once again, taught private lessons, and performed in different venues as well as with a renowned pianist.

Life was often full of challenges, twists, and not always easy in Angels growing up years. In a bizarre incident, two men dressed in suits knocked on my upstairs apartment door as Angel and I pulled into the parking lot. I sensed trouble. I called out to the men to come down as I sent Angel up to the apartment. I instructed her to lock the door and call the police if I wasn't up in ten minutes. The men flashed badges and said they were detectives. I sensed they were not. Angel and I had just returned from doing our morning "bagel run". We picked up large bags of bagels from local shops in town, bagged them, and distributed them to the homeless. With a cheerful grin and a perky expression, I asked, as the men approached my car, "Would you like a bagel, sir?" "I hand out bagels to the homeless, sir." The two men looked at each other bewildered as they looked at the large bags of bread that filled my car and said "No" And turned and hurried away. I called the local police. They had not sent anyone out to my home. Another bullet dodged. A perky, bubbly, almost silly persona was *a Kill it with Kindness, always a card in my deck that played well.*

Angel and I were used to weathering the storms of life by now and were barely getting by financially. Surviving on Social Security and living frugally, I had never worked full time. I had been doing some substitute teaching in the public schools and was occasionally sent to substitute in hospital settings for children and teenagers. A position in one of the facilities in the girl's sexual abuse unit at a hospital became available. I accepted the position out of necessity. At the age of thirty-five, I was, for the first time, doing what many single mothers must do to support children—work full time. This position was unfortunately the second shift, but it allowed me to get my foot in the door. I would work until a day shift opened for me. It would be close to home, and Angel, who was sixteen, assured me she would be fine. I came home for breaks and made frequent phone calls to her. She always made me proud with her sense of responsibility, strength, courage, and resilience.

It was time for Angel to spread her wings and function without my constant supervision. However, it was an adjustment for both of us. I worked hard. Utilizing the alcohol and drug counseling license earned in Iowa, which was recognized by the State of Oklahoma, I developed, implemented, and facilitated a Drug Awareness program for the unit.

It was an interesting place to work. Something dramatic was always happening, and it wasn't always good. When the alarm sounded in the facility, I joined other staff members as we ran in the direction of the incident to form a people pile on top of an out-of-control teenager, an unfortunate protocol at the time. We held them down until a nurse came to give them a shot. I was never comfortable with this choice of restraint. In another incident a child in isolation had smeared blood all over the walls—not a pretty sight. Units were often out of control, and drama a frequent occurrence. Trauma, turmoil, and theatrics fostered intense daily events. Staff shortages, inadequate training, use of restraints, and the precarious feeling that a riot could break out at any time left me fearful and hoping I would make it through each shift without injuries.

I pursued other jobs with better hours, salary, benefits, and conditions. Before long, I moved on by accepting an opportunity as a child advocate with Domestic Violence Intervention Services (DVIS) in Tulsa at the women's shelter. I could author a book on everything I learned from my work at DVIS, but for the purpose of this memoir, I'll just touch on highlights of my work there.

No domestic violence had ever occurred in my home while growing up. Nor had I been in a relationship that included domestic violence, although my husband had been affected by abuse in his home and had described it to me. I couldn't understand why a woman would stay in an abusive relationship. Nor could I understand why a man would hurt a woman instead of just leaving. I could neither conceptualize the choices nor relate to the behavior when I began working there. Was it a mental illness, a bipolar episode, drugs, or a pattern they witnessed in their home growing up that normalized the behavior? Over time, through this work, I came to understand the psychological nuances that drive abusive behavior and why victims responded the way they did. This awareness was invaluable in that job and served me well in later ones as my career progressed.

My job at DVIS was purposeful, rewarding work. I developed and implemented an assessment questionnaire and utilization of the Substance

Abuse Subtle Screening Inventory (SASSI). These were tools that screened people admitted to the shelter for drug abuse problems. Addiction is a major contributor to abuse. These tools facilitated our ability to move people into programs that helped them.

Through the experience at DVIS, I learned about the cycle of domestic violence, the power and control wheel, victim and persecutor roles, and various types of abuse including verbal and emotional abuse. I learned about the devastating, lasting effects domestic violence can have on children throughout their lives. One of the consequences of chronic exposure to domestic violence as a child can ultimately be homicide or suicide. *Was my husband's death a direct result of his exposure to domestic violence in his home?*

I experienced rough spots on my journey after Bodie died because I harbored anger for what he did. As I became aware of the consequences of parental domestic violence, I finally understood why he did it. I let go of the anger that filled my thoughts of him—my poor sad, damaged Bodie—and developed a sense of deep compassion for what he had endured as a sensitive child. And I understood, finally, what shaped him. I once heard it said that damaged people are dangerous because they know they can survive anything. That was not true in Bodie's case. Some do not survive their past.

I embraced working with the children at the shelter. Many came in with nothing but the clothes on their backs. Children are shaped by what they observe from their parents, and they repeat the violence cycle. Girls typically take on a victim role, and boys take on the abuser role. I learned that intervention is the only method that will, in time, free a relationship of domestic violence. I learned how hard it is to change a habit, a pattern, or something learned as a child. And I learned how devastating it is to everyone involved when that change does not happen. Recovery takes time, often with setbacks. It requires considerable self-awareness and a sincere, determined desire to change. And it takes counseling.

I am grateful for all I learned from this organization, one devoted to helping families and saving lives. The experience healed me, and I became determined to be an advocate for victims of domestic violence, male or female, no matter where my career path took me. This knowledge proved invaluable when I later worked for the State Department of Human Services—a twenty-three-year career supporting families.

With this fulfilling DVIS position and Angel and I grounded and secure, life was good. I adjusted to my responsibilities and increased in skill, knowledge, and professional credentials. I loved the people I worked with and particularly looked forward to holding group events with children at the shelter. I spoke at community functions on the effects of domestic violence on children and led teddy bear drives. I knew what I did was purposeful work. I mattered. I made a difference.

I reached out to the church of which I was a member for an opportunity to do a teddy bear drive for children who often arrived at the center with nothing but clothes or pajamas on their backs after a domestic violence incident. A teddy bear meant everything to them. Their eyes switched from fear and panic to surprise as they reached out to clutch onto something soft and comforting.

I was well versed in this presentation, which I had given many times around the city. When invited to speak to a luncheon for a large women's group in that church, I was excited to bring my message to them. The event was a success. The ladies came through and filled my car with teddy bears for the children. All was going well until the tables turned. A shooting arrow headed my way, one that struck me right in the heart and changed me forever.

It was a sunny afternoon, a perfect Oklahoma day. I arrived home from work and sat down to open the mail. What I read stung. A letter altered the course of my life and changed my perception of religion forever. Little did I know that my teddy bear fundraiser would be the last time I would set foot in that church or any other like it.

The experience can be described as nothing less than an awakening. I read the letter signed by the senior pastor of the church. In disbelief, stunned, and shaking, I tried to absorb its content—to digest the malice it conveyed. The letter referred to my seven-year membership with the church and stated that I was no longer welcome there. In fact, not only was I not welcome, but I was not to tell anyone and not to return. It further stated I was uninvited, and security measures would be implemented to keep me away. Astonished beyond belief, I felt physically ill. The shock was like spotting a tarantula in the bathtub.

What was I supposed to think, or do? *I just got kicked out of church.* The letter went on to say that I worked for DVIS, which conflicted with the scriptures that require wives to submit to their husbands. It claimed that DVIS was sending men into exile for petty disagreements and "minor abuses." In addition, it accused me of blasphemy and hypocrisy while doing my job there. Really? *Ouch.* It was as though someone had punched me in the gut. Although it was a hit, I was astute enough to know I was being abused by this church, and I was having none of it. I had observed firsthand what DVIS did to protect mentally and physically abused parents and children as well as its efforts to help abusers. No way would I accept, or cower to, this ridiculous and bewildering religious rhetoric.

Shaken, I considered how getting unceremoniously kicked out of a church would give my parents a heart attack—if I told them. So, I didn't. I never told them. They had been through enough on account of me. I called a friend instead and read her the letter. She was furious and hell-bent on calling a local news station to suggest they go to the church for a news clip. I fought hard to stop her. I didn't want the news and cameras showing up at the church and causing a stir in the community or involving DVIS.

I called my boss at the agency, who was equally astounded and said the agency would back me if I wanted to take some kind of action. I wasn't sure there was a viable legal action for outrageous religious beliefs. However, even if there were, the answer would be "No." Neither my daughter nor I needed the stress. We had been through enough and I wanted nothing to do with that church—ever. I just wanted to get away from its awful creed and ridiculous, dominating patriarchal position. This was a situation that warranted me simply taking my marbles and going home.

I knew instantly my relationship with the church was not redeemable under any scenario. Nor was it possible for me to influence its leadership's interpretation of its religion. I recognized the irrational absurdity of their position and the implausibility of them ever becoming enlightened. *The person who wrote that letter must live with himself and answer to God. And Karma can be a bitch!* Although the incident weighed heavily on me, the message from their volley was disgusting, and I wanted nothing to do with that church, anyone in it, or any church like it. Sadly, misogyny prevails in some quarters of religion and women, children, and men pay dearly for it.

My boss at DVIS called the pastor about the letter and the church's position on domestic violence. I enjoyed the church leaders knowing I didn't comply with their demand that I not talk to anyone about my expulsion. *You are not the boss of me.* I'm certain that phone call made the pastor squirm as he was forced to recon with the seriousness of his action. When confronted, he called the letter "bogus." He denied writing it and even went as far as to say I was welcome in the church. *No, I am not. Clearly, I'm not, nor would I want to be at this point.* I believed he was lying. In fact, I was certain he was. He was a coward. When it came to sticking up for his religion's creed publicly, he caved.

The letter was written on church letterhead. My personal membership information was accessed to produce the letter and send it. Membership information was kept in the church office and not accessible to just anyone, the letter was signed with the pastor's signature. If he didn't write it, someone would have had to gain access to my personal information and forge his signature—an unlikely course of events.

The pastor's cowardly response and subsequent inaction on the matter re-confirmed my belief that he was the culprit. If he believed his lie, he would have searched out and exposed the culprit, secured membership information, and followed up with me. And, he would have given me an apology. He did nothing. He was probably laying low, hoping the situation would go away, which it did, for him at least. Frankly, I didn't care what he did or what happened at the church regarding this issue. I had experienced a fundamental flaw in religion and its teachings, which ignored rational thought, crushed critical thinking, and endorsed a patriarchal doctrine harmful to families. I was done with him, his church, and his kind of religion—one that endorses domestic abuse. That letter introduced a defining moment that changed me forever.

Not every problem can be solved. Sometimes, it is better to walk through the harshness of life and move past the incident. Taking vengeance doesn't heal the wound, nor does it erase the offense. Rather, it often magnifies the issue and leads to further devastation. Someone wrote that letter, and that person must answer to their Creator for doing so. I would not fight this war.

I had devoted myself to this church. I had taught Sunday school and volunteered for vacation Bible school. Angel had grown up in the church where she participated in youth group activities, was the star vocal soloist on Christmas Eve, and was the church scholarship youth award winner for college. I would not be a good mother if I allowed her to be involved in an organization that supported women submitting to violence and abuse.

Avoiding that sort of religion was an easy decision. It is disturbing that such an injurious event was an easy choice for the church. Kicking a young widow woman out for collecting teddy bears for children exposed to violence—come on now. Who does that? An incident such as this would never have happened in an Iowa church.

I vowed to take the church's lesson to heart. I shared the letter proudly, even framing it in gold and hanging it on the wall of my *hall of fame* next to my degrees and credentials. I dusted myself off and never returned. By walking away from those bitter, ridiculous, fake Christians who were affiliated with that so-called church, I found a better path, a more righteous one.

CHAPTER 12

TIME TO LAUNCH

PURPOSEFUL WORK COMES AT A PRICE

An intense restlessness set in at my job at Domestic Violence Intervention Services (DVIS). I was hungry—ambitious. A desire to provide a better life for my daughter and to find an organization that offered upward mobility, and benefits compelled me to move on. My credentials and experience qualified me to work at Child Welfare Services for the State of Oklahoma. That was my goal.

At DVIS, I was required to report allegations of child abuse. So, I interacted with state child welfare workers who came to the shelter. They had cars, cellphones, and laptops. Job security, good benefits, and opportunities for advancement at a state position were also attractive. Although apprehensive about pursuing a serious career, I felt compelled to try; it was time to launch.

In 1995, and despite the advantages of state employment, the notoriously bad reputation of the Department at the time disturbed me. The work included excessive workloads, extreme work demands, inadequate funding, staff shortages, and worse yet, poor outcomes for citizens. But in the interest of perceived opportunities, perhaps the change would be worth the risk.

A four-month application process seemed to never end. At last, I secured an interview that took me to the office on 36th Street North, a predominately black part of Tulsa. Although the city was vibrant and rich with modern culture, a racial divide lingered under the surface, exacerbated by an unfortunate racial incident in the early 1900s that left a mark on the city.

I will never forget the day of the interview. With courage and fortitude, I headed to the office, dressed to shine. To appear professional, I wore a navy blue suit and matching navy heels. With nails manicured, make-up applied, hair up, and notebook in hand, I pulled into the parking lot in a car remarkably nicer than others in the lot. An audience of tall, rather intimidating black men hanging around outside the front door stared. My presence got their attention. I wondered what I had gotten myself into. I was so uncomfortable that if I still smoked pot or cigarettes, I would have lit up. As a finished-off, blonde-haired person from South Tulsa—a predominately conservative part of town—dressed to the hilt, and driving a Toyota Camry, I was out of my element and felt out of place.

Having never been outside of my own neighboring vicinity, I was shocked when I pulled into the parking lot and spotted that gathering of curious men staring at me. Who were these men? Were they staff or clients? Why were they congregating at the front of the building? No doubt, they were wondering: *Who is this woman and what is she doing here?*

Cigarette butts and trash littered the parking lot. I wished I could park behind the gated lot with a sign posted: *For Employees Only.* I glanced around at the considerable number of rundown cars and hoped mine would be safe. Everything about that environment was unsettling. Panic set in regarding my appearance. I was a princess. Feeling uneasy, I took off my earrings, watch, and bracelets; toned down my lipstick; wiped blush off my face with a tissue and wished I had worn more practical shoes. My jacket would have been abandoned had it not been required to shroud a thin silk blouse.

I took a deep breath, reviewed my notes, and talked myself into leaving the safety of the car. Acting purposefully, I walked through the parking lot and up the stairs, acknowledging the men as I navigated through the group. "Good morning, gentlemen." Their responses were mixed—a couple of robust "Good mornings" and a few snickers and elbows to the ribs.

Seated in the lobby among clients waiting for their appointed turn to apply for food stamps and other means of financial assistance, I was the only white woman there. Most adults appeared to be indifferent to others in the room. I smiled at the few who gazed at me, obviously as curious about me as I was about them. Bashful children stared and grinned when I flirted with them. Others fussed, cried, and ran amuck.

My name was called, and the receptionist took me back for an interview with two fabulous, impressive black women who would eventually mentor me and have a significant impact on my career. I got the job; however, the location would be at this 36th Street North office, and the position would be in the Department of Temporary Assistance for Needy Families. It was obvious from the interview and the location I was assigned to that this would be a tough gig.

The women who hired me took a chance on me—possibly betting I wouldn't make it. And for the first time, I had a serious, purposeful career with benefits and potential for advancement. My status at the agency sparked envy from other workers because I entered at Social Worker II status. A new hire at that level was unusual back then. Coworkers questioned me about this. I let them know I had a degree, thirty hours of graduate work, a license in alcohol and drug counseling and had worked at DVIS, all of which bumped me up in classification. I had paid my dues. That settled the matter.

On the first morning of my new job, I punched my alarm clock, got my butt out of bed, dressed casually, and made the long drive to work in rush hour traffic to interject myself into an uncomfortable environment. Intensely motivated to give my best to the job, I hit it hard. This change introduced a major shift in my life as I aspired to chart a serious and productive career path for the first time.

As a young widow living on Social Security while raising a daughter after my husband's death, I stayed home for sixteen years except for part-time jobs. Content to live a frugal life based on simplicity, the focus was on raising Angel. I didn't need a lot to be happy. Embracing a career with a new and more fervent sense of responsibility and serious professional goals would require a demanding lifestyle shift as well as a fresh perspective. Nonetheless, with underlying feelings of inadequacy, which I pounded back into the recesses of my mind, I put on my big girl pants and embraced the challenge. A sense of adventure stirred as I headed to work that first day. Little did I know what lay ahead.

I learned quickly and mostly from the women who were my clients. In fact, we learned from each other. When talking with one of these women about the prospect of her finding a job and getting off welfare, she said, "You don't understand." I responded, "I may not understand what it is like to be on the same assistance you are on, but I have been in a similar situation. My husband died when I was nineteen. I had no skills, experience, or education to get a good job. I raised my daughter on social security. (I didn't tell her about my stripping job.) During those years, I got a scholarship to go to college and furthered my education. At the age of thirty-seven, I started my career, and that's why I'm here today. If I can do it, you can, too." She recognized the commonality, and I gave her hope.

Or did I? Looking back on that scenario, I realize my story was not hers. I had family support and never lived in poverty. She was in a generational system of social services that left no quarter for one generation to support another or for becoming educated and getting ahead in life. Now, I realize the grandiose illusion and naivety of my perspective. She was not like me, and I was not like her.

I had compassion for her and her struggle to care for her children alone. She had no transportation, relied on the city bus, no parental support, and an absent partner. She cared for five children under the age of eight years old while doing her best to navigate an inadequate, unwieldy system. I do believe my encouragement helped this mother and others like her to some degree. We connected, and I softened her world with social services support and a personal interest in her and her situation.

The kink in the prospect of a rally for her included numerous social barriers: Who was going to take care of her children while she got a GED and furthered her education? How was she going to navigate multiple children attending different schools with different schedules, and how would she secure transportation? There are programs for some who qualify for childcare, but they are inadequate. Who would stay home with her children when they were sick? How would she obtain job experience? Could she qualify for a college scholarship? Bottom line, she had no safety net except for government assistance.

Therein lies the crux of the problem of generational welfare—a lack
of adequate support, finances, and education. In addition, there were
persistent cultural influences and a legal system that incarcerated many
black men, leaving women alone and bound to government dependency.
Drugs and guns prospered in poor communities. Too many young men's
careers included selling drugs, and their futures included incarceration.
Too many young men had guns, and they killed each other in shocking
numbers, thereby decimating families. Police don't deal much with fights
anymore. They investigate homicides. This situation exists even to this day.

The welfare program in Tulsa was severely broken at the time.
Understaffed and underfunded, I and other case managers worked hard.
With over four hundred cases at any given time, long days and excessive
overtime were routine. One never had a sense of completion. It was run,
run, run. After a couple of years of frustration with the futile nature of the
situation, a restlessness stirred, and I explored options to promote to other
divisions in the agency. Child Welfare was an option. I believed children
were resilient and given proper care, able to overcome their circumstances.
Perhaps I can do more good there. I also hoped to get a job in the downtown
office, closer to home, with better pay, and lunch options rather than
brown bagging it in a neighborhood with little food service. I applied for a
lateral move to the downtown office as a Child Welfare Specialist and got
it. Workmates told me I would be sorry and warned of the homes I would
have to go into alone in rough areas of town. My response was, "I will find
out for myself." After weeks of training, I was ready to chart my course and
do just that.

My workmates were right. Nothing could have prepared me for what
I was about to walk into in the field. What I found was not good.
Children endured disturbing circumstances I could not have imagined.

That propelled me into action. It was not possible to save all the children, but I did what I could for those poor, darling little souls whose hopeful big eyes looked up at me and stirred me to action during the day and gave me bad dreams at night.

Days turned into nights and weeks into working weekends. I had thought work at DVIS was a challenge, but that was nothing compared to the twenty-three years I worked for the State. The experiences would leave a mark, but despite the overwhelming challenges, I discovered what I was born to do. My traumatic past of fixes and failures that had made things worse for me toughened me, taught me hard-learned lessons, gave me empathy for the desperate and downtrodden, and steeled me for the job at hand. I had found my niche.

The agency at the time was burdened with a substantial backlog of cases. I was sent out to check on a teenager who had been reported as suicidal a year ago. No one had gone to check on this child. *Why now? Why me? What would I say? "Is your son still alive?" What if he had passed away?* I must have had a look of acute anxiety on my face when the boy's parents opened the door. Relieved to learn the child was okay, I made inadequate but honest excuses for the department not responding in a timely manner.

There were other such incidents. In fact, a few thousand backlogged cases existed at the time that no one had responded to. I was in shock and disbelief as my workload grew with more cases than anyone could manage. In addition to the volume of cases, the emotional anguish they generated stunned me. *Could I handle this?*

I teamed up occasionally with a male colleague—my deskmate. One cold, snowy day, I was uncomfortable with making the drive to a client's home and asked him to go with me. He had good navigation skills, valuable in those days before GPS technology. I, on the other hand, often struggled with reading maps and finding my way around the maze of poorly marked enclaves in and around Tulsa. After making the long commute and finally locating the correct address, we arrived at a trailer home nestled in a woodsy area.

We walked up dilapidated wooden steps and knocked several times on the door with no response. Disappointed with our efforts after making the treacherous drive, we turned to leave. I slipped on ice on the stairs, landed flat on my back, and slid down into snow and dirt. I wanted to cry. I was a mess—dirty and hurt. I could hardly walk. Back at the office, my supervisor mandated that I fill out Workman's Compensation paperwork. As I healed, I was overwhelmed and frustrated with the bureaucracies of that system. But I soon recovered, escaped the paperwork and procedural madness, and went back to work.

Shockingly, I eventually lost my deskmate after he became hostile because I wouldn't go on a date with him. That's all I needed. This situation piled onto another layer of stress. I had no intention of ever going out with him and made that clear. He responded in a negative manner, making it impossible for me to continue working with him. I kept a journal record of all interactions with him and continued on until I was able to move to another desk.

Although this employee relations issue added to the stress of the job, it was working in the trenches with children and families in the depths of despair that eventually broke me. I was a tough gal, though, and it took twenty-three years to do so. Although I had been through a lot in my life, I had never experienced the conditions, violence, disdain, poverty, and deplorable, heart-wrenching situations I faced on this job.

After the early years of being a victim and in more recent years of seeking salvation for my unfortunate behavior, landing this job produced a defining moment that changed everything. It turned me into a rescuer. Rescuing was a tough gig, but I relished the role, dug in, and worked hard for the children and families in Oklahoma. As a result, my confidence blossomed. I made a difference—all day, every day—and I knew it.

Working within the limits and internal constraints of the system was a challenge. Court and police mandates—at times punitive, yet necessary—impacted the work. Although restricted by these requirements, discretion was applied when possible. Educating clients on the underlying causes of their situations rather than focusing solely on dealing with symptoms produced long-term rather than short-term solutions. Families are the fabric of our society, and I wanted them to be the best they could be—to be resilient, to have pride, to face adversity with their heads held high, to believe they could do better, and to take command of their lives. I wanted children to feel safe, secure, and nourished. I wanted parents to avoid feeling stigmatized. I wanted them to put pride aside and overcome their hesitancy to ask for help. I wanted them to be okay.

People often asked me back then—and still do to this day: "How could you do this work?" I asked in return: "After what I saw, how could I not?" Although much of my initial motivation for seeking this work was economic security and career advancement, what kept me going was a sense of purpose and making a difference.

Although my career was challenging, it was packed with rewards. Driving home from work, I often contemplated what would have happened if I had not showed up that day. Could there be any more purposeful work than to relieve the suffering of a child, to make a family stronger, and to help others who needed a hand? I hung in there for years. And I was good at what I did.

As vital as my contributions were, though, they left a mark on my psyche. Years of potent exposure to vicarious trauma resulted in compassion fatigue and secondary traumatic stress. Eventually, I suffered symptoms of PTSD.

CHAPTER 13

IN THE TRENCHES

IT'S GONNA LEAVE A MARK

F ew people are aware of the despair and suffering that goes on behind
closed doors. Those on the front lines of law enforcement and social
services face that reality daily, and they protect the rest of society from its
assaults on the human condition. A harsh reality was revealed when I lifted
the veil on tragedies and horror that caseworkers observed firsthand year
in and year out. The reality of those revelations was shocking. Intense and
horrific suffering made the work tough, traumatic, and at times dangerous.
Perhaps I hung in for so long to achieve recompense for my unfortunate
behavior in my younger years. But, mostly, I did so because once I saw the
madness, I felt compelled to stop it. Of course, I could not. I did make a
difference, though. I walked into the trenches and did what I could do.

The situations revealed here were real. Children, the most precious gift
in our society, were impacted in ways most people cannot imagine. Their
plight fostered nightmares and sleepless nights for me. Twenty - four
hour on - call demands, and thirty- six-hour shifts added to the stresses
I experienced for over two decades. Recalling those experiences now is
emotionally painful, but they represent a major portion of my life, and I
would be remiss by ignoring them in my life story.

I saw maggots in refrigerators several times. And I can't forget the smells, nor can I describe them. Such things are real to me. Hauntingly real. Some of them are common and I saw them over and over. Others are shocking. All are real.

Each situation was approached with determination and fortitude; however, my life was laced with tears from experiences that invaded my head at night, keeping me awake. As I sat in church, these thoughts hovered in the recesses of my mind. Also, the unfortunate plight of so many young children haunted me as I nurtured my daughter. I carried the burden of a heavy heart, knowing that many children did not receive what I worked hard to provide for Angel. But I endured.

CHILDREN SUFFERING

A newborn baby coming down off crack, a baby life-flighted with a skull fracture, a disabled child with roaches in his tubes, a child made fun of at school for smelling like feces because sick and diseased dogs lived in the home. Walls smeared with feces. A child with the only place she didn't have scars from abuse was on the bottom of her feet and genitals.

A two-pound baby fighting for his life because of a mom with poor nutrition, nicotine use, and inadequate prenatal care. A young child being starved and wearing infant-size clothing. A teenage girl living alone downtown in a tent. Children going to a convenience store to wash up before going to school. Meth-positive babies, children drowning, starving children, and children alone in cars while parents gambled and drank in casinos all hours of the night.

Cigarettes extinguished on children. A child made to wear soiled underwear on his head. A child who wanted to die, an abandoned boy with nowhere to go, too many children without beds, and a toddler wandering alone on a busy street in diapers. Pills, knives, and chemicals on floors where toddlers wandered. Burns and more burns.

A child's father on death row. Children defecating in cans in the backyard because of no running water. Crying babies and crying mamas. Children sleeping with roaches crawling on them. Lice crawling on children's heads. Abused babies. Pregnant young girls. Children with conditions whose parents failed to follow through with needed medical care. A child provocatively posted online.

DESPERATE AND DEPENDENT MOTHERS

A mother freaking out on meth; another feeding her addiction by taking her child's life-saving medication. Yet another taking her child's Foundation money to purchase drugs. Mammas trading their children for sex acts to feed drug addictions. A mother abused to the point of near death going back to her abuser. Odds were, she was going to die. A mom and three hungry children with nothing in their apartment but a mattress.

DADS BEHAVING BADLY

A teenage boy witnessing his dad holding a gun to his head and threatening to commit suicide. Dads threatening to kill their babies' mamas. A father teaching his son how to steal. A man forcing his partner to shoot meth into his penis by gunpoint. Parents' religious beliefs preventing them from seeking medical care for their children.

A child disclosing her stepfather sexually abused her. A young boy told me his stepfather anally raped him as I interviewed him at school. A mother and child I had desperately tried to save were murdered. I carry that horrific incident with me to this day. A child was stabbed with a knife by his father's girlfriend. A girl was sexually abused by multiple family members. A girl sexually abused by her grandfather. A baby thrown against a wall. A child permanently disabled from abuse.

DRUGS

An active meth lab in the home and forty pots of shake-and-bake in another. Shake and bake is a method of making methamphetamine without a heat source. Drug cameras on homes and vicious dogs chained to front doors or running amuck in yards. A baby dead because her parents rolled over on her while passed out on drugs. Gangs, drugs, guns, and violence. A machete beside a line of cocaine spread out on a cabinet. Parents passed out on drugs while children wandered outside unsupervised. Too many drug-positive newborn babies to count. Children exposed to drug use or poisoned by the manufacture of drugs in the home. Terrified children clinging desperately to parents who abused or neglected them when the police and social services come to rescue them.

DEPLORABLE ENVIRONMENTAL HORRORS

It was bad enough that Pit Bulls, loose dogs, snakes, and reptiles threatened me, but masses of mice and rats were a menace as well. Thirty mice were flushed down a toilet in a mouse and rat-infested home. A mouse ran around food on a kitchen counter. Mice crawled on children while they slept. I dodged mice playing on the floor. Pet snakes, pet rats, and pet iguanas ran loose. Severe infestations. Roaches falling on me.

Empty cupboards and refrigerators with hungry children hovering about, their eyes pleading for help. Maggots in refrigerators—really. Homes littered with condoms and sex toys on the floor. Floorboards caving in throughout the house. Homes with no electricity or water were common. A home with an offensive odor so pungent I couldn't enter.

DANGER AND VIOLENCE

Fifteen police officers lined up behind me on the stairs of an apartment complex while I knocked on one door. Standing by as a police officer drew his gun to try to gain access to a home to check on the safety of a child. A man answering the door wielding a baseball bat. A man screaming at me, one inch from my face, demanding to know who reported his case, which is confidential by law. I inched my way toward an exit while a leering, threatening drunk demanded I come closer as he perused my body. I entered a home to discover an alleged perpetrator with a loaded gun next to him in his chair. How did I know it was loaded? He told me. In another case, I froze and backed away slowly, one step back at a time, after encountering a mentally ill man in a rage.

***

In addition to all the human issues, the social system was broken. Babies were not provided adequate identification. One of my workers called me in the middle of the night to tell me she had given parents the wrong baby. The infant was in DHS custody and was being returned to their custody. The worker was handed the wrong baby by the placement provider. The police went with us to make the exchange. This was a delicate situation with the potential for negative outcomes for the babies, both sets of parents, and the agency. The baby that was mistakenly given to the wrong parents was cocaine-positive and experiencing withdrawals, which complicated the matter. Needless to say, new protocols were implemented in the county after this incident.

Children abused in homes were often neglected or abused in foster homes as well. And there were not enough homes for children taken into custody. One of my workers had to stay the night with a child in the office because there were no placements available. I cried because this was the ultimate failure, and was chastised by my boss for crying.

I had to plan arrangements with funeral homes to bury children who died in state custody. How many babies and children can I mourn? Some were lost from sickness, some from neglect and abuse, and others from accidents. Occasionally, a baby or child was murdered. I conducted a funeral service for a child who died in State custody, and in another case, I had to ask a church for a pastor to bury a child. I planned funerals, spoke at one because no one else was available, and stood at gravesides and wept, sometimes with family and other times with members of the community. Police detectives assigned to cases were at times present out of reverence and sometimes to ensure that alleged perpetrators didn't show up and cause trouble.

Numerous times, when I thought I had seen it all, even more shocking reports of abuse or neglect crossed my desk. Such situations invaded my personal life. It was not unusual for notices of horrific abuses to be conveyed to me while out to dinner, at a church function, or on the way to a social event. More than once, I had been awakened from a deep sleep and notified of a child who died.

I ask myself, if I had realized going in that I would be intimately involved in burying babies and exposed to criminals and nut jobs, would I have done it? Or would I have pursued other options? I honestly can't answer that question. At any rate, those experiences are a part of me now. I don't know what to do with them. But they are there—still.

Many of my experiences in the trenches exposed the depths of inhumanity—the despair, desperation, and deprivation I didn't know existed. These revelations took their toll. I struggled against becoming desensitized as I observed other workers doing so. I desperately tried to take away the pain of sufferers, but interventions often failed. Irreparable damage had been done to many people before I entered the picture, and not every horror could be fixed. All I could hope for was just to somehow make situations better.

How can one be adequately prepared to go into a crack house, a meth lab, a gang-ridden neighborhood, or a rat-infested home? What can prepare a person to talk a mother out of killing her child or to deal with a child telling you his father sodomized him? Overseeing such incidents was not something I was taught in school or in the Department's nine weeks of classroom training. And the cases kept coming—day after day, year after year—accumulating into a mass of turmoil buried deep in my mind.

In addition to emotional stress from the situations encountered, pressure from the threat of legal consequences from my decisions was ever-present. What if I made the wrong call? In one case, as often happened, a mother cried as she told me why and said she worked long hours, two to three jobs, and didn't have time to properly take care of her home and her children. Given the age of the young children and the unsanitary conditions in which they lived, this would have ordinarily prompted the removal of the children from the home. But, as I often did, I gave her a chance after observing her tears, hearing why, and sensing her truthfulness. "I'll be back.

I want it cleaned up," I said. I inquired: "Who is your support system? Who can help you?" She said she had help. She also had me. I was on her side.

With the children living in this situation, I was taking a risk by not taking them out of the home. I was accountable to the State for their welfare and, according to policy, it could be concluded the children should have been removed. Still, I made the call and gave her time to remediate the situation. If something happened to those children during that time, I would have been held accountable.

There were always underlying conditions of some sort in every situation I encountered, sometimes drugs or mental illness. This situation seemed different. I returned to the home two days later. To my surprise, it was clean and organized. The woman had even shampooed the carpet. I was aware that it does no good to correct such conditions if the person goes back to the same old ways—another thing for me to worry about. I told her that if the next time I visited I found the same deplorable unsafe conditions, I would most likely have to approach the District Attorney's office to request the children be removed. To avoid that prospect, I developed a plan and wrapped community services around her.

I wanted to know why people were in the circumstances they were in. Rarely does anyone contemplate why. I wonder what would happen if more people took the time to ask why instead of judging and applying quick fixes. I always asked that question because no one ever asked me why when I was running away from home. If someone had, things might have been different.

So many cases touched my heart like the child I had to take out of his home because he was disabled with a tube that had roaches in it. I tried to understand how this could happen. Why? My conversation with the parents revealed the father's dilemma. He said, "Joan, we have not had one eight-hour night of sleep since he was born." The child was now ten. And so, we located resources in the community to help so the parents could have respite and provide for their child's needs. Eventually the child was returned to his parents. This case inspired me because of the positive outcome. That was not always possible.

At the end of the day, I did my job while teaching the families to use the tools I provided, to access community services and providers, and to reach out when they needed help. I did my best to follow Agency policies and procedures as well as laws while serving families. The progress gave me a sense of closure as I shifted my focus from one family to the next. I remained hopeful I could leave families in a better position than when I found them, and sometimes I did. Sometimes not. There were many tragedies. My path to making a difference and surviving was to focus on positive outcomes. Many people inspired me as they responded to the help offered to them. Others disappointed.

What I experienced made it a challenge to remain positive. The disturbing reality that I could not fix everything was disheartening. I wanted to see little girls wearing pretty dresses and their hair neatly done up in bows. I wanted the boys nicely groomed, with haircuts, and wearing collared shirts. I wanted children to have more than one pair of shoes. I wished for happy children playing, growing, and living with nurturing loving parents in a perfect family. In so many cases, that was impossible. I struggled with such realities in the situations so many children faced.

I teared up when I saw children at church nicely dressed. My first response to observing children who appeared cared for was to feel badly about the underprivileged children I touched day after day. Then another gremlin took over my thoughts as I entertained the notion that even those children in church dressed in their pretty clothes may not be okay. That kind of thinking reflects the consciousness of someone who has seen and experienced too much.

I was conflicted many times by the tasks I had to perform. Dark interpretations hovered like angry demons over my thoughts. How many times could I wrangle an at-risk, sobbing, clinging child in imminent danger out of the arms of a hysterical, screaming mother before cracking. The memories took their toll. It was not unusual for me to cry while driving home from work. Eventually, I broke. It was time to save myself, which brought me another fail in a long string of fixes and fails. I failed at getting out of the fray, which was my loss. The Oklahoma child welfare system failed as well, and many people paid a severe price. I could only do what I could do, and so often, that was not enough.

Children of the Night

In the noonday and in the darkness of the night, I see the fear in their eyes
as their souls find the courage to fight and to hope.
One more story, one more night, can I be the person who will make it right?
A child, holding her teddy bear tight, tucked in and saying good night,
spreading her wings for flight or another night of fright?
One more story, one more day, and one more night holding on with all
their might and hoping I will be their hero who will rescue them tonight.
I look into their pleading eyes and smile. Later, I cry.

Joan Sandergard

CHAPTER 14

A FIRE IN THE BELLY

TIME FOR HIGHER GROUND

The primary purpose of my job with Tulsa County Child Welfare in 1997 was to protect children from abuse and neglect. Most often, the abuser was a parent. It was heartbreaking to observe such cases over and over, and the work took me down another road of torment. In my conversations with abusive parents, the correlation between the disciplinary practices they used and how they were raised became evident. Generational abuse was often identified as a major contributor to mistreatment, and breaking abusive patterns was challenging. Parents often were not aware of the damage certain forms of punishment could do to a child, such as the use of an instrument to punish. And they were unaware of laws that were implemented over the years to protect children from abuse. When parents learned they could no longer leave marks on their children, the use of alternative methods of discipline didn't come easily.

Observing abuse firsthand created layers of anguish when I was exposed to helpless, innocent young souls being physically and mentally scarred for life. Their little minds and bodies were so battered there was little doubt that their lives would be changed forever by verbal, and physical attacks.

Working for years in this venue often left broken little people, a broken system, and eventually, a broken me.

After two years of working on the child abuse investigations, a sense of restlessness intruded, and I looked for a way out. I became determined to move out of the front lines of welfare service and climb higher in the Department. This was primarily because of tiring of the anguish, but innate ambition was also a driving force. Once secure in an organization with numerous avenues for advancement, I chased those opportunities. Why I was so ambitious and aspiring to move up was—and still is—a mystery to me. No doubt the nature of working in the trenches was a factor. I was always looking to escape, but each position generated its own form of hell. As it turned out, I didn't escape the field work with this promotion either, but I did move up to an elevated position as a lead child welfare worker.

This position came with a new set of challenges. A delicate job with a specialized caseload, it involved working internal investigations on DHS employees and others who worked in agencies and organizations that collaborated with the Department. This included police officers and people providing foster and adoption homes. My caseload also included an assortment of complaint and compliance cases. Responsibilities covered a four-county district across Oklahoma. In a building away from my peers to ensure my independence, I collaborated with a team of my superiors. This was a step up from the previous work environment—or so I thought. Turns out, the job did involve fieldwork. It seemed as though there was no escape from being thrust into emotional affronts.

Not knowing if I could do the job—or like it—I did what I had always done. I dug in and went to work. Sadly, in this new position, I discovered some children in the custody of the State for abuse by their parents were now being abused in foster homes. This reality sickened me. I had placed children in foster homes in my previous position. I was naïve. When I learned about the extent of abuse and neglect that happened to children in State custody and often for the same reasons they were removed from their parents—the reality of that atrocity hit me hard and left me disillusioned.

Like with previous fieldwork, I was assigned to investigate reports of alleged child abuse and neglect, covering a broad four-county area. Come rain or shine, I was sent out on cases in rural counties. I was back where I started, tramping around in obscure, remote places, dodging dogs and an occasional enraged man and dancing around mice and cockroaches. Geez. These were homes on country roads with no street signs or house numbers in a time before GPS technology was available. Directions might include "Turn by the big oak tree," or "We're in the back of the green trailer house," or "There's a large rock on the corner." Roadkill was splattered on winding, narrow country roads. Aggressive, loose dogs frequently greeted my arrival.

Feelings of hopelessness again invaded my thoughts. Still, I continued, even though I was exhausted, overwhelmed, and overworked. A familiar option stirred in my mind. It was time to get out of the field for certain and continue the climb to higher ground.

***

I applied for a supervisor position over Child Welfare Investigations. Dressed in my navy suit, head high, and with luck on my side, I landed the job of Child Welfare Supervisor. This was unheard of, I was told.

Most people applied several times before getting this position. The same concerns I wrestled with at each rung of the ladder haunted me. What if I cannot do this job? What if I don't like it? What if I embarrass myself? I didn't want to let people down who believed in me. But again, I did what I knew to do. I had been overwhelmed in past positions and always prevailed eventually. With determination and a strong work ethic, I buckled up and prepared to tackle the beast. I hit it hard.

Life took on a new direction as I functioned as a supervisor. I worked in a building in East Tulsa, one I refer to as a rundown shack. Abandoned refrigerators and condoms littered the parking lot. Bubble gum machines from storefront robberies were strung about, and water dripped down wires inside the building. Large ice mounds surrounded the parking lot in the winter. Due to being a high-crime area with few desirable lunch spots, I brown-bagged my lunch most days just as I did in the early years. It was as though I had fallen back to where I started, but I had become accustomed to unpleasant working conditions. At least I was not being chased by dogs or threatened by angry men in the field. And experience had taught me that I may not like my job, or even be able to do it, but I would, as always, give it my best shot. And that I did.

I worked long days, nights, and most weekends. Surmounting pressure ensued in the reality of this new position. As a middle-management employee, the circumstances surrounding my job were only somewhat improved. I still carried dog treats to distract aggressive loose hounds and pepper spray in case of aggressive loose humans, but most of the work involved leadership of a team. As it turned out, this was my forte. The position was a good fit.

Management skills came naturally to me. I was responsible for five to seven employees. Struggling with upper management issues introduced stresses, and pressure from families in unfortunate circumstances continued to weigh on me, but leading a team to deliver results was a worthwhile and fresh experience, and it made me feel as though I had found my niche.

With an innate drive to organize, manage, and administer, I discovered the power of leadership and synergy and tapped into my staff. They had considerable potential, which had not been harnessed. I encouraged teamwork, pulled them out of a victim mentality, and instilled in them a can-do attitude.

My boss expected zero backlog, but no plan or strategy had existed to make that level of performance possible with overwhelming caseloads. So, I developed plans, improved processes, and established goals and standards. The work required considerable stamina, but I was accustomed to that. With my daughter raised, I was fully committed to work. I focused on outcomes and results. By developing and capitalizing on the talents of the staff and establishing procedures and processes to facilitate their work, a higher standard was set, and amazing accomplishments were achieved. Instead of feeling like victims of the work environment and a flawed system, they became winners who took pride in their purposeful work, overcame obstacles, and made things happen, and made a difference.

My staff were selected to provide a presentation to the Commission on Human Services, appointed by the Governor of Oklahoma to provide oversight for the Department of Human Services (DHS). It was an honor to be selected out of a four-county district, and one well-deserved as we had met our goal of maintaining zero caseload backlog. Together we developed a presentation detailing how those results were achieved. We gave credit to community partners by including interviews of them in the presentation.

Despite all that progress, some days I felt stuck. Employee burnout and turnover were high in this type of work. The money was not good, the pressure was intense, and long days, nights, weekends, and on-call availability were required. I often didn't do well with the bureaucracy of the state, including the laws, protocols, and changing policies that governed the Agency. To complicate things further, legislators frequently inquired about a decision my staff made on cases, which required further investigation and my written responses. This was important work, but it added additional pressure and distracted from the work required to facilitate employees and to get the job done for the Agency. I was in a constant state of being pulled in different directions.

The prospect of making a wrong decision was a continuous threat; however, I always knew that policy was my friend. If I followed the State's policy, it would be on them if something bad happened. This was an uncomfortable reality. Nevertheless, stamping my approval and signature on an average of one hundred child abuse reports a month to be forwarded to the District Attorney's office was required, and I would be responsible for risky decisions based on gray areas in policy.

Knowing I made a difference kept me going as did career achievements. I was awarded the Fly Like an Eagle Award for the superior performance of my staff. I excelled at investigations and frequently testified in court cases. I was qualified as an "expert witness" for the court due to the high volume of investigations I had worked and the knowledge I had gained in the field.

We had triple the workload by today's standards and significant staff shortages. The agency was overwhelmed and soon the consequences of that would become public. Funding and budget issues, political oversight, and management issues all plagued the organization, resulting in too many children in custody, negative outcomes, and excessive burdens for front-line staff. The system was severely broken and had been for some time.

In 2008, an out-of-state advocacy group sued DHS over deficiencies in the system. The Federal Government stepped in, and a Federal Action Lawsuit cited that there were too many children mistreated and dying while in DHS custody. A settlement agreement was reached between the Federal Government and the State of Oklahoma in 2012, and the Department underwent a paradigm shift. A plan was implemented to improve the lives of children and to create child welfare reform. Increased State funding and Agency appropriations resulted in lower caseloads, pay raises for staff, home-based services, an increase in foster homes, and other measures to improve outcomes for Oklahoma's vulnerable children.

Why did it take a Federal intervention for DHS to take better care of Oklahoma's children, families, and its employees? It was a toxic and dysfunctional system at every level with millions of dollars in lawsuits awarded to plaintiffs in compensation for injustice, harm, and at times, death to children. These problems were exacerbated by Oklahoma politicians' unwillingness or inability to fund education. To this day, Oklahoma ranks as one of the lowest states in education and healthcare.

It took a small advocacy group out of New York to come to Oklahoma and make a difference. When all this happened, I was at the pinnacle of my career and was afforded opportunities to share my knowledge and expertise with a number of affiliates and agencies. I spoke to organizations and conducted training and in-services to groups ranging in size from 5 to 150 with a wide variety of audiences, including Rotary Club, Court Appointed Special Advocates (CASA), Sexual Assault Nurse Examiners (SANE), The Health Department's Children's First Nurses, University of Oklahoma (OU) MSW students, numerous in-services at schools for teachers and counselors, The University of Tulsa (TU) law class, Victory Christian Center, TV Network; Joy in Our Cause, and many more. I even spoke once to a group of OB/GYN doctors about sexual abuse of children. I had to wonder: *How does a degree in Elementary Education* and all those courses in *theology prepare me for this?*

One thing I could always count on with the Department was change. After a re-structure and the establishment of zoning within the division, I moved to a more centralized location with better accommodations. I welcomed the change and the better working environment. However, after twelve years of supervising for Tulsa County, mental and physical threats, and exhaustion hovered. I had a sense of becoming desensitized. Additionally, chest pains and concern for my heart weighed on me. So, I strategized on ways to get out of the fray.

I applied for a trainer position in the Department where I would be responsible for training new Child Welfare hires. I landed the job, but my excitement over the change was short-lived. It was a misstep. I had traded one problem for another. This was not a good match. To get out of the situation, I would most likely have to step down to a lower-ranked position. But, sitting in my office one day gazing out at the sky, a thought impressed upon me. I was going up the ladder, not down. Returning to fieldwork was intolerable. I believed that if I did so, I would become completely desensitized or go bat-shit crazy. I advocated for years, and I couldn't do it anymore. I could not experience one more investigation of traumatic child abuse. Secondary trauma from chronic exposure to horrific events had already set in, and I was done.

I decided to apply for a District Director job in Tulsa County, an administrative job with oversight for Child Welfare Planning. I knew little about the job; however, I did know it was a move up and a brighter side of Child Welfare. It involved working with parents and the court system to get children back home after their removal. Reuniting families instead of breaking them up was beyond enticing. It was salvation.

I applied for the job and was accepted for an interview. Preparing for the most critical interview of my career, I spent hours studying, researching, and reviewing talking points. I developed a portfolio for the interview panel. The written portion of the interview required a response on balancing accountability with staff development and employee morale. My management experience paid off. I knew this part of the job well.

I was fortunate to have had many wonderful coaches and leaders in previous positions. I learned to lead with efficiency, energy, and a standard of excellence. I had made tough decisions, executed good judgment, tapped into resources and the innate skills of staff, and sustained positive outcomes for children. I knew a team approach was a successful building block to success. Additionally, I championed examining biases and valuing cultural diversity. I had knowledge of the Child Welfare organization and the laws and policies that regulated it as well as an awareness of community needs. And I had a proven record of delivering results.

While preparing for this interview, I became convinced that this position was the perfect match of my skills to the job. With the ability to lead and to adapt, I developed a vision of what this position required—most importantly the need for collaboration with community partners and the installation of necessary checks and balances. The day of the interview for District Director of Tulsa County Child Welfare came. With a portfolio for each panel member, I interviewed for what would be the last time in my career. This came one week before a trip I had planned to Switzerland with my mother. The timing could not have been more perfect. I was either going to celebrate the new job with my mother in Switzerland, or stay in Europe, elope, and not return. Well, maybe not elope.

I waited. Then one night the phone rang. I accepted the offer. I would return from Europe going full circle to where I started my Child Welfare journey in 1997, only in a much higher position, one in which I could have influence on a broader scale.

I worked as a District Director for five years during which I had oversight for seventy employees. I was responsible for cases assigned to baby court, drug court, permanent custody cases, and Independent Living, a program for youth aging out of foster care. Hiring, instigating corrective discipline, and terminating employees when needed were my responsibilities. On call twenty-four seven with little life outside of work, I was married to my work and dedicated my life to it. At least I wasn't facing child abuse cases every day.

I could write an entire book about my career. It was a profound chapter in my life's journey. Repeatedly I forced myself out of my comfort zone and into new challenges and finally arrived at a high-level position of influence. It was lonely at the top. Internal and external pressure, critical negative personalities, changes of the guard, no homes for children, outside stressors, exhaustion, and the inevitable and constant challenges took their toll. My ambition got me in over my head several times, but with grit, determination, and occasionally some "fake it till you make it" gall, I accomplished the tasks.

Four years into this last position, I sustained significant back-to-back personal losses that introduced deep grief. This included a love of thirteen years who suffered a terminal illness and died. Shortly thereafter, my mother died. It was time to retire. And so, I did. With over 1,200 sick leave hours and the maximum of accrued unused vacation hours, I said goodbye and left the State building for the last time in November 2017.

It was a privilege to have served the State of Oklahoma. I did so in many capacities over the years. In addition to formal responsibilities, I served as a board member for the Tulsa Advocates for the Protection of Children, and was a member of the District Attorneys task force, the Oklahoma State tribal group, the Child Trafficking task force, and the Child Protection Coalition. I left it better. I mattered, and I left a mark on the Agency.

As I look back on my tenure in child welfare services, I realize it was the one–on–ones with children and families as an investigator that was the most rewarding and where I did some of my best work. I still miss that essential challenge. But other forces presented themselves, including financial need, the punishing emotional toll of observing abuse, and-admittedly-ambition. One reason I survived as long as I did was because of what happened outside of the work environment. I found love. An enchanting distraction that carried me through for thirteen years. Then I lost that love followed by the loss of my mother. Those losses left me alone and devastated.

Prior to exiting the Department, I enrolled in the Employee Assistance Program to transition from the agency—to diminish the prospect of carrying secondary trauma into retirement. I had gone into the belly of society and endured twenty-three years in that environment, inviting those there to walk with me as I showed them a better way. I championed learning among those who didn't value it. I had influence and my life counted for something. I changed lives, but I paid a price for that. It was time to debrief and heal.

CHAPTER 15

A COSTLY FAIL

SOCIETY'S COMPLEXITIES—SOLUTIONS ARE POSSIBLE BUT UNLIKELY

Examining life choices from a distance years later with a fresh perspective, I think about society's complexities and the welfare system that brought me to a state of considerable despair. Behind the veil of American society and at the bottom rung of its culture, the downtrodden exist. Among those unfortunates are children. Dysfunctional families abound. My career spanned twenty-five years of work in domestic violence prevention and child protective services for the State of Oklahoma. I saw situations few people could imagine and lost hope on the part of suffering citizens. Government regulations often failed and contributed to the perpetuation of problems.

Issues of the legacy of welfare flowing through generations and other social ills are multi-faceted, and the solutions complex. Inequity of socio-economic status, political unrest, religious and cultural differences, mental health, drugs, and poverty are deep-rooted, long-standing problems that deliver severe negative consequences. My experience while working within the system and observing the political environment on which it depends suggests there are actions that would redeem, or at least significantly improve, the situation. Unfortunately, they require social and political paradigm shifts, an assessment and revamp of the system, and cohesiveness between federal, state, and locally funded programs. That is a big order.

I had a rough beginning in life, although not to the degree of most of the clients I served while working for the State. What saved me from the fate of many clients was that my family was able to avoid poverty. Additionally, I refused to give in to hopelessness and sought out education as the path to recovery. I aspired.

Few parents I worked with in the welfare system had any sense of aspiration and most of them had lost hope, or never had it. They saw no way out of their plight—no path to improving their lives. These factors are major contributors to generational welfare.

I loved the people I worked with who struggled for generations, for one reason or another, and were unable or unwilling to go off welfare assistance and gain employment. What were the barriers? Lack of skill, education, healthcare, confidence, fear, mental illness, drugs, domestic violence, childcare, incarcerated parents, or entitlement? Yes, all of these. But also, the system that perpetuated these factors was and is the root of the problem.

So often, no one asks why. The root causes of the problems require an understanding of why. No one consciously aspires to live a life of poverty or sets this as a life goal. Unfortunately, people on welfare are often harshly judged, misunderstood, and criticized. It reminds me of when as a teenage runaway, no one asked me why.

When I first started the job as a social worker for the Department of Human Services, I was unfamiliar with the realities of the welfare system's policies and laws. I eventually learned about them and the circumstances that promoted hopelessness and contributed to fostering the predicaments of the people the agency was commissioned to serve. There were many social drivers, and these influences were complex.

Whatever the reasons, I always believed in the best of people, especially the women with children, who struggled against the tides of welfare legacy, many of whom were abandoned by men who were incarcerated, or victims of unfortunate cultural influences. These women grappled with the failure of public assistance programs. Could they be the ones to stop the generational dependency on government assistance? Yes, but the solutions were profoundly problematic and unlikely to happen.

Imagine politicians of today reaching a consensus on doing something for the people. Too many are preoccupied with personal goals of power and greed and getting re-elected. They are more interested in divesting themselves of helping others than investing in workable solutions. There are cost-effective, doable solutions, but few champions to advocate for them.

When I worked at DHS, the system designed to help these people was broken as evidenced by how many adults and children were beaten and violated; the number of dysfunctional families desperately needing rescue; and the number of babies and children I mourned. The damage was broad and deep and often unrepairable. I tried to make sense of it all. Why do people get into such desperate situations? And how can the system help them? Or can it?

For many families, perks of childcare benefits, transportation, and educational assistance could offer paths to economic sustainability. Additionally, affordable housing could redeem families and decrease homelessness. Introducing remediation programs rather than incarceration for minor crimes could reduce the number of fatherless and motherless families. A shift of funds from legal enforcement to treatment for alcohol and drug abuse could promote better outcomes at less cost. Enhancing prison reform through rehabilitation, educational programs, and mandatory mentoring programs could lower the recidivism rate and help reintegrate citizens back into society. Increasing mandatory treatment for nonviolent drug and alcohol-induced crimes, rather than fining and jailing people for an illness, could help. Increased funding and programs for mental health services and family planning could have a profound impact on improving lives, supporting families, and reducing violence.

These viable solutions could make the country stronger and more economically sound. Resources could be directed at helping people become productive citizens who pay taxes, rather than people who drain the economy by relying on welfare, impede law enforcement, and end up in prisons. Attempts at dealing with gangs, guns, and crime have not worked. These are solvable problems inhibited by an unfortunate set of priorities embraced by politicians corrupted by flaws in democratic processes.

Legislators hesitate to embrace the morality of taking care of people—such as in the case of school shootings—while they eagerly apply moral and religious judgments to other issues that hurt constituents and exacerbate society's issues. Too many legislators' priorities are driven by corporations, the wealthy, and greedy power seekers. Our political system is broken, and our democracy is at risk.

I struggled with the Government's role to regulate and intervene on a non-criminal level in families' lives and at the expense of the overburdened multifaceted system. Does the Government make better parents?

Children are removed from homes for abuse and neglect that often reoccurs in state foster homes. Children are abused at an alarming rate, and some even die in foster care. I knocked on the door of a biological mother to tell her that her child had died in a foster home leaving her too destitute to function. I arranged the service and spoke at the funeral while desperately struggling not to cry. This experience prompted more questions, many with viable answers that were unlikely to happen.

More preventative programs to educate boys before high school and college about healthy boundaries, dating, and potential consequences of their behavior could help mitigate potential problematic situations. With computers, and cellphones wide open, even internet nannies cannot keep our children safe. They are exposed and groomed at an alarming rate.

Although some suggest that if churches and charities did their jobs there would be no need for social services. These organizations are disconnected, not robust enough to solve such immense problems, and hampered by ancient creeds. Additionally, they don't have the finances or resources, nor can they coalesce because of disparate beliefs into a cooperative unit capable of managing the task.

Why is it that some states suffer with alarming statistics and others have higher standards of education and healthcare as well as decreased crime, incarceration, divorce rates, teen pregnancies, and violence to women? Are there community, religious, cultural, and economic factors that influence social norms and politics? What reforms would encourage citizens to regain hope and aspire to a better life?

America is in a downward trend and children are being killed at an alarming rate. These problems will continue unless our leaders focus on humanity.

I was often asked how I could work for so many years on the plight of the neediest in society. My career was challenging, but it was also rewarding. I gave my best every day, and my compassion never wavered, though fatigue and mental stressors were constant companions. Making a difference motivated me.

I may be out of the trenches now, but I am not out of the game. Although it is unlikely this country will find its footing, reset its priorities, and make significant changes in its political system and social programs, there are opportunities for progress. I learned through my work that one person can make a difference. My retirement plan is to do so. Like in John Fogerty's song *Put Me in Coach, I'm Ready to Play, Today,* I'm all in if needed.

.

CHAPTER 16

LOVE HAPPENS

A Diverse and Splendid Landscape of Suitors

Throughout forty-five years of being single and dating, a charming landscape of men crossed my path. I was not deprived of love. I enjoyed several deep loves and romances throughout the years and experienced one true, long-term love. My efforts at seeking connections produced many types of love: fun, needy, smitten, healing, exotic, and most of all crazy, wonderful love. Being single for so long fostered love for different seasons and reasons.

Not all suitors came with a solid moral compass, or reasonable intentions. For the most part, though, love was a blessing. Eternally optimistic about affairs of the heart, I looked forward to who waited around the corner after every breakup—someone to walk with me and help me on the next leg of my journey. And I was eager to help him as well.

Like the butterfly I chased as a small child, fabulous men landed for a while and then fluttered away, or I did. They warmed my heart and left me with memories of love lost—sometimes painful and sometimes not so much. Regardless of the circumstances around the end of these relationships, I was a better person because of each of them. We were all flawed, them and me, but whatever the circumstances, I was the beneficiary of their love, and each one left me with a lesson learned from having known them. In every case, I wished them well in the end, and still do.

Loves came and went, but one thing was certain. Once I rallied from my teenage traumas and early twenties, my daughter was number one in my life. I didn't date much during Angel's growing-up years and rarely brought men home to meet her. I protected her from exposure to anyone who would not be a mainstay in our lives. Once she was raised, though, I did some serious dating, which was mostly a good thing although occasionally a bad one. Dating and love was a complicated process wrought with unpredictable outcomes.

Despite those reservations, I often had a man in my life after Angel was raised and had left Tulsa to go to college in Dallas. Although I stumbled through a couple of losers, most were exceptional men—kind, giving, outstanding men with a lot to offer. And I know, because of my reticence to love again, I hurt several of them. Damaged, with a complicated history, I could only go so far into the realm of romantic love before I panicked and bailed.

Earlier foolish years included colorful, interesting, and brief relationships: one with an Elvis impersonator—really, a tennis instructor, a short-stay live-in, and others. A more sensible choice was a romantic church love I met right before I got sober.

When not in a relationship, I dated casually. This involved many Saturday night salmon dinners as I sat across the table from a man with both of us seeking a connection. This often involved a blind date, which, as we single people know, can go either way, but most often poorly. Fortunately, with the Internet, the risk of that is reduced. With all the resources available online, it is difficult for people to hide the truths about their lives.

Seven men proposed marriage—an arrangement I avoided, and I'm glad I did because I knew I had a long journey to heal. And I never met someone I wanted to bring into my daughter's world. I didn't trust love would last. I floundered around in the romance arena while avoiding anything serious. However, love is a persistent pursuer, and like a river, it flowed through my life.

In later years, when I had embraced an all-consuming career, new platforms and venues for dating developed and new relationships surfaced. I dated a man of the church during Angel's senior year in high school and later was involved in a one-year relationship with a man wounded with a broken wing I sought to repair. He flew away when he was healed.

I searched for my former ORU flame from thirty years ago, Dr. Boaz. I found him living in Canada. He was in the process of going through a divorce with a woman ten years his junior with whom he had three children. He was broken. That made the prospect of reconnecting implausible. He had a solo journey of healing to walk. Boaz still had a piece of my heart.

A five-year relationship with a Federal Agent who was an ex-military man and decorated with honors, was an easy comfortable, but intense love. I met him while on jury duty, and we dated after Angel had left for college. We were good for each other until our lives took us in different directions. The breakup produced an excruciating goodbye, but because there was real love there, we both wanted the best for each other, and we let go easily.

As wonderful as love was, dating was plagued with downsides and, in some cases, potentially dangerous experiences. The fact that I endured all that and still sought love demonstrates considerable tenacity. I hesitate to put a negative spin on love by referring to the downsides, but by not doing so,

I would be lying by omission. The process of finding love is complicated and messy.

I experienced too many tongues with a first kiss. Too often fine dining was interpreted as an obligation for sex later. Too many times a lack of chemistry killed the deal. And too many unfortunate characteristics plagued the landscape of men: dominance, poor boundaries, cognitive deficits, missing teeth, self-absorption, and one fellow who asked on our first date if I wanted to get drunk.

As I got older, many men in my age group chased younger women. As a result, they had immature, or even psycho ex-wives and were saddled with alimony and child support obligations until they died. And, no doubt, if I fell for one of these fellows, his history suggested that at some point he would leave me for a younger woman.

Searching for love was like searching for a seashell in the sand. There were plenty of them, but few worth taking home. Without love, I was unanchored at times—drifting and harboring an unfulfilled longing. Although I had many captivating and special experiences, as a single woman, I accumulated a substantial number of lessons learned from experiences in the arena of romance. I list the more interesting ones here to share some of those lessons:

TRUST YOUR INTUITION

The most important indicator of a winning relationship is how the person made me feel. Some people are sweet talkers. It was important to remember that it is what they do, not what they say, that counts.

Trust must be earned, not assumed.

A few men were downright scary. An unplanned walk with a fellow on the first date ended up on a trail in an unpopulated area, which triggered my intuition. I ran.

On the news, I learned that a man I had dated was arrested for a terrible crime for which he was later convicted and sent to prison. I dodged that bullet. Trust must be earned. I learned to exercise healthy skepticism when considering who to bring into my life.

A college professor and photographer admitted to me at dinner that he paid women to pose nude so he could photograph them in poses, including yoga positions. *No downward dog for me, baby. This date is over.* I worried about his students.

People lied on the Internet about their age, whether they smoked, and often posted misleading photos. A guy might not be smiling in an online photo because his front teeth were missing. Interestingly, people who lied on the Internet complain that people lied on the Internet.

STICK TO YOUR VALUES

A man bragged, "My former girlfriend was eight years younger, and sex was hot." This reflected a lack of good judgment, which left me cold.

A fellow who lived on a yacht with a hot twenty-one-year-old visitor staying with him revealed he was looking for an open-minded woman—a co-captain to live on the seas. Nothing good could come from such an insensitive man.

Another flaunted his fortune. In fact, that was all he talked about. He even discussed his estate on our first date. This red flag suggested incompatible values.

A friendship with a brilliant, kind, giving and successful older man was enjoyable until it became evident he wanted more. He took me to fine restaurants and other venues I had never experienced and sent a landscaper to my home to plant a garden of flowers in the yard. He had a singer in a club sing *You Are My Sunshine* to me. However, when the friendship escalated and I knew there was no chemistry, I bailed. I could not take advantage of his generosity once I realized his expectations. I had adjusted to a frugal lifestyle many years ago, and material possessions were not that important to me. If someone is crushing on you it is difficult to maintain a friendship. At some point, friendship is going to hit you on the lips and paw you like a bear.

NOT A GOOD MATCH

An adorable country cowboy and police officer in strong pursuit wrote me love letters and invited me to horseback ride across France. That could not be romantic to me in any sense of the word. I was not a country girl. I was accustomed to heels, not boots. *In these heels? I don't think so.*

Police officers, SWAT team members, detectives, firefighters, coaches, athletes, military guys, and other tightly bonded men have friends who you must win over. A short-lived affair with a swat team police officer, owner of an arsenal of guns and ammunition, left me with an appreciation for those who put their lives on the line every day for others. However, I had to realize a relationship with one of these men was like dating a band of brothers.

DON'T MEASURE UP

A fellow's back-to-back DUIs and a recently revoked license taught me to research each prospect before dating. I was up for a reformed alcoholic. Shoot, I was one. But someone in the throes of this problem needed to be avoided.

Doctors, lawyers, financial executives, property owners, and other well-to-dos seemed like a catch, but some were fresh out of a divorce and not ready for a relationship; or the IRS or creditors were chasing them.

It was an insult when a married man thought I could be interested in him. One man took his wedding ring off during our date. I learned to watch for a visible suntan line that suggested a missing ring. I considered it a violation of sisterhood to consider such a man.

NARCISSISTIC OR CONTROLLING PERSONALITIES

They were often charismatic and charming at first, engaging in love bombing in the courting phase. This included gifting with extravagance, wining and dining, excessive admiration, and devotion. Those behaviors would change. Extreme jealousy, rushing the relationship, attempts to isolate me from friends and family, and building me up and then tearing me down were red flags.

On a first date, before I was aware of this personality type, I was gifted with a pair of exquisite earrings. Within two short months of dating, the guy wanted to marry. Also, he tried to monopolize my time and didn't respect my independence. These were red flags not to be ignored. When they appeared, I did not worry about hurting someone's feelings. I bailed. The longer I would have stayed in, the harder it would be to leave. Not only would it be extremely hard, but it could possibly even be dangerous.

I had a two-year, off-and-on relationship with a man who lived out of state. The first time we got together, I was led to believe we were in a relationship until the visit ended, after which there was little to no communication. I was not desperate for a connection, so I moved on to other possibilities.

Sometime later, he showed a renewed interest in me and invited me to visit him at his Florida home. We had a wonderful time together. Again, I believed we were in a relationship until that visit ended, and again all communication stopped. I wrote him off for good. However, he returned sometime later pursuing me aggressively. He came to visit me in Tulsa. This time we decided we were boyfriend and girlfriend until he left, and communication faded even though he had invited me to visit him in Florida and booked a one-way plane ticket. Shortly thereafter, he canceled the trip.

I concluded he was courting me between girlfriends, or he had made up with an ex. I felt "played." I received an email in which he said he assumed I had wanted to move in, and he was not ready for that. That was ridiculous.

He had invited me and bought the one-way ticket on his own. He was projecting his bad behavior onto me. Can you say *gaslighting?* He said, "I hope this does not end our "special" relationship." *It was not so special, and his actions did end it.* I ghosted him. I should have reacted earlier to obvious red flags. Two days after that, I had someone new to date.

Quality men were in short supply. The good men were taken. Divorced men were broke and broken; wealthy men endeavored to steal my independence; country boys gave their girlfriends NRA t-shirts and took them to Bass Pro-Shops for entertainment; young men offered jalapeño poppers at Sonic for dinner, and great sex on a futon; men were inclined to leave a woman for a younger one, unless they are shopping for a nurse; and the rest just wanted to do my hair.

Despite the downsides of dating and relationships, an undeniable force propelled me on a quest for love. Losses made that journey hard, but with each relationship, I learned, grew, and had few regrets.

Some loves were transient. Although they left a mark, they were paltry in comparison to the forever kind of love that invaded my soul, stirred my senses, and left a tattoo on my heart when the loved one was gone. Nevertheless, forever love was worth the effort required to find it and the price paid to experience it.

The price of love was the thorns, the tears, and the good-byes. Twice, love brought me to my knees, but I became wiser for the failed attempts at seeking it. With resilience, I continued to hope for love.

CHAPTER 17

THE DANCE OF LOVE

A FINE, FANCIFUL ATTACHMENT

As my career unfolded in earlier years and finances were still tight, I secured a second job with Ralph Lauren as a fragrance model working at local department Stores. The seasonal work was enjoyable. I dressed up, donned fashionable hats, and wore pretty clothes. Working with the public was a positive experience in contrast to my job at Child Welfare. Happy children came into the stores dressed up and anticipating Christmas. Meeting people was the best part of the job. Occasionally, I would see friends, or someone from work, but nothing could have prepared me for who walked up to my counter on December 24, 2000. I was working at the Dillard's counter in upscale Utica Square when I looked up to see a familiar face—a judge I knew from representing child welfare cases in his courtroom.

"Hello, Judge," I said, "Merry Christmas!"

He smiled and replied, "Merry Christmas," obviously as surprised to see me as I was him in a setting outside the courtroom.

A striking, distinguished man, he was well dressed as always but without his judicial robe. I was not wearing my typical work attire either. Dressed fit to impress, I was dolled up in full makeup, including red lipstick, and styled hair. I wore a red and black Christmas suit, fashion hat, hose, and high heels.

His face lit up with a broad smile and twinkling eyes.

"How are you?" I asked. "Can I help you find something?" "Yes," he said, "I am looking for something for my mother. She likes Mackie products."

"Okay. I can make her a Christmas basket while you shop. However, the shelves are nearly empty. It is Christmas Eve day, and products are practically sold out." He told me to put everything I had left in the Mackie line in the basket. I was elated about the big sale, especially since only high-end items like real perfume and luxurious body cremes remained in stock.

Meeting this impressive man under these circumstances reminded me of how much I had admired him when observing him on the bench. I had been doing so for some time. Actually, I was crushing on him.

I watched as he picked up a couple of designer handbags and other items off the shelves until he was out of sight. A man who bought his mother the absolute best with no regard for price was impressive. *She must be incredibly special to him,* I thought as I went to work making the most elaborate Christmas basket ever, wrapping it with an ornate bow. I wondered who the handbags were for.

The judge returned, flashing a big smile that revealed white teeth gleaming in contrast to his ebony skin. Obviously pleased with the basket, he wished me a Merry Christmas and went on his way. I watched him leave with his hands full of bags, but stopping to put money in the bucket for the bell ringer in front of the store. Tall, handsome, and oozing a profoundly powerful bearing, he disappeared from my sight. *Merry Christmas, indeed.*

My heart fluttered. My spirit and senses stirred. Clearly, he was attractive, but after this experience, I concluded he must be an exceptional person as well. I was reminded of how he fascinated me in the work environment. His masculine voice, tall stature, and chiseled face were captivating. And the man had style. A penchant for suspenders set him apart. His eyes pierced through me in his courtroom, and my eyes shined and danced every time I saw him. *Be still my heart.* My forbidden crush continued—hopelessly. Yet I remained thankful for the connection that Christmas Eve day.

The holidays came and went. With the New Year, opportunities for fresh beginnings were on the horizon. I couldn't get the judge off my mind and remembered something told to me years ago: "Go after what you want." I wanted him. So, I did just that. Brazenly, I decided to step out of my comfort zone and send him a note.

Should I address the note to the courthouse? Hoping I would not get into trouble, I mailed a notecard to "Your Honor," telling him I hoped he had a good holiday, and that his mother loved her basket. I also wished him a Happy New Year, and at the end, I added: "If you ever go out with white women, I would love to do lunch sometime." As a single woman for many years, I had dated several men, but I was never that forward. Each one was special in his own way. This man was different. He was worthy of me taking a risk and making a forward gesture.

The holidays were over, and I went back to work supervising Child Abuse investigations at the East office. It was a new year and time for new dreams, a new vision, hope, and perseverance. Sitting in my office one snowy day, I turned on my computer to find a slew of emails. One caught my attention. It was from Kian, the judge. Ecstatic, I opened it.

He thanked me for the note, and said, yes, that he did go out with white women, but that he was currently seeing someone. We agreed to keep in touch, though. I took another risk and told him I would love to have lunch sometime if time permitted.

We began meeting for lunch occasionally. Thankful for the transition from work colleagues to friendship, I valued our connection. Since my job changed and I was no longer in his courtroom as a worker, our lunches seemed appropriate from a professional perspective. I was pleased to connect with him on a personal level, especially since I admired him when I was a worker in his courtroom. Always with a spark in his piercing eyes, he was vibrant and exceptionally skilled at discerning the truth. That quality was particularly appealing to me because competence was something I always admired in a man.

I respected his honesty about dating someone else, which spoke volumes about his character. I wondered about that relationship, but since he never talked about the subject, I chose to put it out of my mind. It was against my nature to pry, and I respected his decision not to bring it up. I even admired him for that.

During our year-long friendship, I learned about his background. With deep roots in the community, his family was well-known and highly respected. His father was a prominent pastor who traveled extensively during his growing-up years. Kian valued family and education. He often spoke in the community and took a genuine interest in others. In particular, he took an immense interest in young people. He cheered on the youth on his docket, even going so far as to attend their athletic and school events. The man was impressive—dignified, cultured, generous, esteemed, and well-traveled. I marveled at the fact that he appeared to find me interesting. I couldn't have dreamed that big.

All was going well with our newfound friendship until one day when he walked me to my car after lunch. I turned to say goodbye in my usual manner, but this was no usual goodbye. He put his arms around my waist and drew me close. His intoxicating scent surrounded me as he pulled me into him. For me, this was the embrace of a lifetime. I had never felt such an intense physical connection before. He pressed his lips to mine as I succumbed and leaned into him. My legs felt weak, but his powerful grip held me up. I was not prepared for what happened and emotions swirled making me feel woozy. My chest—pressing against his—buzzed as if butterflies fluttered inside me.

This moment charted a new destiny for me. When I leaned back, our eyes met and locked together in an intense and knowing gaze. He explained that he was single and free. To me, this was an offering from the universe, and I was grateful he was still holding me up. Otherwise, I would have surely dropped to the ground. In that moment, our spirits and souls intertwined, then merged. And so, our dance began.

***

In his apartment days later, the judge took my hand and asked me to dance. The music played as we turned to each other, and our bodies began to sway. We danced in his high-rise apartment with the lights of downtown Tulsa twinkling through the windows. The moon shone into the dimly lit room and stars lit up the sky. He held me close, leading me with smoothly executed turns and reversals. As we became accustomed to moving in sync, he twirled me around under his tall frame. Our bodies moved in unison, and I followed his lead easily as though we had danced together many times. The outside world faded away, as did the events of the day. I nestled into his arms. Eventually, our movement slowed until, motionless, we hugged for what seemed like forever—our bodies blending as one. In this blissful moment, there was no doubt but that we were falling in love.

I know that bliss is something that happens only in the moment. It is not sustainable. But for thirteen years, Kian and I would experience it over and over until a finale I could never have predicted changed the trajectory of his life and mine forever.

CHAPTER 18

CROSSING THE CULTURAL DIVIDE

LOVE THAT CANNOT BE DENIED IS DENIED IN THE END

My love had arrived, a great love—a deep, passionate melding of souls that lit a flame that burns to this day. That fire would change everything for me. I was alone, and Angel was living in Dallas, so love came at a perfect time. Kian and I instantly connected on multiple levels—something I had never experienced before. Our interactions ranged from continuous banter and flirting to deep discussions about careers, families, dreams, ambitions, and intensely meaningful social and intellectual subjects. And the attraction was off the charts.

Kian loved talking about his family, and he spoke fondly of his son. And he adored his mother. Family was everything to him. Taking an interest in me—my family, my history, my dreams—he sought out details of my life story. Listening intently to every detail, he made no judgments when I candidly revealed my early troubled years. I showed him my soul, my foibles, my embarrassing fixes and fails, my accomplishments against all odds, and my joys and heartaches. He took it all in, his eyes revealing his interest, his laughs appreciating the humor, and his hugs showing his compassion and support. I could tell him anything. I never held back. And he loved me still.

With a staunch belief in the good in every person, Kian was a realist—a judge—who had seen the bad in people firsthand. Yet, somehow, he reconciled the good and the bad and found a way to champion everyone. In doing so, he made a profound difference in people's lives. He mattered. He left a mark on everyone he met. Highly intelligent, intuitive, and a gifted conversationalist, and people gravitated to him. He was everyone's champion. He believed in the possibilities of redemption from human error and the value of education. And he was a black man who broke barriers at a time when that rarely happened. In addition to his professional accomplishments, he devoted himself to making a difference in the lives of others. He encouraged underprivileged people, especially the young. A generous contributor to charity, he was a particularly enthusiastic advocate for a cure for Sickle Cell Anemia.

Kian was a man worth knowing and worth loving, and a man who knew how to love in return. What we had was a great love. Tall, dark, and extraordinarily handsome, with eyes that sparkled, he possessed a powerful, confident, and manly countenance. The appeal was irresistible. His intelligence was attractive to me since I admired that and competence more than any other quality in a man. But, like every human, Kian was flawed. He struggled against the currents of change, which did not come fast enough for him. Thirteen years after we found love, he would acquiesce to the lack of societal progress, and the consequences of that would leave me damaged.

Kian and I had profound respect for each other. Our focus when we were together was to "just be" after long difficult days at work. We relished every minute of our time together. I lightened him and he lifted me up. Together we soared. He championed me and had my back. We "got" each other and related on every level. We laughed at the same things. Our values were in sync and our compatibility limitless. We never argued, not once. We discussed personal and professional issues, current events and trending stories, politics, and religious issues, and always agreed on what we thought was right. I did become upset with him twice, but to no avail. On the first occasion, he knew I was upset and invited me over to his place so we could talk. By the time I got there and nestled into the sofa, he turned to me with those alluring, twinkling eyes, and asked, "What do you want to talk about, dear," as he leaned over to kiss me.

"Uh, nothing. I forgot," I responded as a smirky grin crossed my face. I surrendered. He had me, and he knew it.

The second time I was upset with him, I arrived at his place, and he had a plush stuffed ladybug waiting for me that said *I love you* on it. My heart fluttered. I reveled in that moment as the thing I was upset about no longer mattered. From then on, nothing upset me, except the demands of our careers that occasionally had me feeling like a football widow because of our grueling schedules. Our time was precious—and ours alone.

The relationship had a natural progression. We were professional colleagues in the first year and transitioned into friendship the following one. That friendship germinated and organically grew into love, fostering a sound foundation. We both had all-consuming careers and worked evenings and weekends. When one of us was wiped out at the end of the day, the other could relate. Talking about work was rare, and it was never a focal point of our relationship, but in a sense, it was the foundation of our compatibility.

We cherished our time together as a respite from the pressures of our careers. We needed that, and we protected it. As we nestled into the partitioning of our public and private lives, we didn't go out with other couples, nor did we involve our families in our relationship. We recognized that, even though more acceptance of interracial relationships had evolved, some people held on to their judgments. Since we were both prominent figures with notable careers, we were determined to keep our personal lives private. We both dealt with people in the community all day, every day, and valued the solitude and quiet times when we retreated to our time together.

We saw no need to create connections with either of our families either. My daughter and her family lived in Texas, and I had no family in Oklahoma. I was unaware of Kian's intentions regarding his family, but I imagined the complication our relationship could stir in a community rooted and scarred by a historical racial divide that traumatized Tulsa citizens. We were different in skin color but one in every other way and on every level. Even with the clever management of our unusual relationship, I often lamented: *Why is there such a deep cultural divide in this country?*

Looking back, I realize that the cultural divide between a black man and a white woman was wide, especially given our respective roles in the community and the fact that Kian had been raised in a prominent and deeply religious black family. He had risen above cultural inhibitors to become a highly regarded success story in his ethnic community. He shared with me his excitement about moving to an apartment in South Tulsa, a predominantly white section of town. For me, this was an ordinary apartment complex. For him, it was an elite establishment that represented his overcoming barriers and having a successful career. With sacrifice and hard work, he had achieved a degree of class, style, and professional success few men ever realize—white or black.

Kian was protective of me and our relationship. The nuances of our careers and lives made our attachment more intense and deeply valued. It was not unusual for either of us to work sixty-plus hours a week. I was on call and constantly interrupted by one crisis or another—serious, sensitive, disturbing emergency calls. I received them when he was at my place or I at his. I would go into a backroom and take the call. Often, they affected me emotionally and would dampen my usual cheerful mood. I quickly rallied, though, when I was with Kian. Such interruptions were one of the reasons we stayed around home and avoided going out. Our time together was often an occasion for introspection and healing because of work issues.

We alternated between each other's homes. I enjoyed cooking and preparing homemade meals for him at every opportunity. He was a meat-and-potatoes kind of guy. I was a salad and veggies kind of gal. A man of prayer, he folded his hands to say grace before each meal.

When Kian arrived, appetizers and snack bowls were on the coffee table, the air smelled of a carefully selected scent, and our favorite soft jazz played in the background. At his home, I lounged while he took care of me, prepared the meal, and did the dishes.

Kian came over after work, always calling to tell me he was on his way. I greeted him at the door. He enveloped me in a supple embrace, drew my lips to his, and sent chills up my spine. He went into my room and placed his wallet and keys on the dresser. A man of order with everything in place, he was notoriously known at work for having an extraordinarily neat and orderly desk. I wondered what he did with all those important legal papers. He was organized, efficient, and always on time—a man who could be relied upon for anything. These qualities were why his behavior at the end of our relationship, which was out of character for him, was such a mystery and a shock to me.

Kian looked for the remote and turned on the television, often watching *Sanford and Son* to laugh and de-stress. I dressed for our Friday nights together, usually wearing something I would not wear in public. Always a sharp dresser, his external presentation reflected sophistication and class, even on our casual evenings. His vehicle was consistent with this persona. He buzzed around town in a classy sports car.

I lived in a basic two-bedroom condominium at that time. A renter all my life, I never owned a home, and don't to this day. He was also a renter, enjoying the convenience of a maintenance-free lifestyle. I had a balcony facing the parking lot, and sometimes I waved to him from there when he arrived. I was excited to see him as he came through the parking lot and up the stairs. One day a little girl, about seven years old, sat out on the balcony next door. She called out to him as he passed her. He greeted her back and waved at her enthusiastically, his delight obvious. He had the biggest smile on his face as he entered the building. It amazed me the extent to which he took a genuine personal interest in people.

Serious discussions were sprinkled between romantic interludes. It was not unusual for us to lock lips and kiss for thirty minutes and beyond—really—without coming up for air. I loved his lips and couldn't get enough of them. It was a time of deep love and spiritual connection, a time to treasure, and a love story.

Christmas was a special time for us as well as birthdays, and most holidays. I noted his six-foot-three stature when I opened the door on Christmas Eve. He stood there with a big smile on his face, holding a small bag from

Moody's jewelry. He did this every year for thirteen years. I always knew it was something special he had picked out for me during his last-minute Christmas Eve day shopping, as he had done for his mother when we met. His gifts to me were big-ticket items in a little bag. My gifts to him were several small-ticket items in big bags. He would stare at the mass of gift-wrapped packages for him under the tree and chuckle. Some Christmas Eves were spent at his home. A neighbor commented that it looked like he was going to have a fine Christmas when he saw me walking down the hall with multiple bags of gifts carefully wrapped. It was always a good Christmas. Thirteen of them.

Stretched out on my sofa with his feet in my lap and no cares in the world, Kian exuded contentedness. With a full belly and after having a few drinks into the evening, he sometimes dozed. I woke him with homemade desserts, often a piece of key lime pie. And then we danced. Our love was one of joy, passion, peace, and contentment. He was everything to me—my world.

Times were not always easy. He experienced significant losses, and I attended three of his family funerals within a two-year span—his mother, his brother, and his brother's wife. I saw the hurt in his eyes. He loved his mother so much and visited her weekly without fail. I had been told that choosing a mate who showed love and respect for his mother and yours was a sign of how you would be treated. His family sent his mother eighty roses for her eightieth birthday. He was close with his older brother who meant the world to him. And he often spoke of his sister, who had died years earlier. These were significant losses that weighed heavily on him. I often played flute for him, hoping the sound of the flute would soothe him and help heal his deep pain, but mostly I sat helpless with him in silence while he gathered strength in solitude. When he reached for me, I was there for him.

Eventually I became concerned about Kian. Intuitively, something foreboding haunted me. I asked him about spots and lumps I noticed on his six-foot-three frame when his long legs were stretched out on my lap. His body was a story, and I wanted to know about each scar, lump, and bump. At one point, I noticed a dark spot under his fingernail. He brushed it off like he did all my observations, saying everything was fine, and it was nothing. He clearly didn't want to talk about any spots on his body, nor why he had been losing weight. My questioning grew old for him, and he claimed that he had received glowing reports from his checkups. So, I put aside looming concerns.

My intuition proved to be correct, though. Everything was not fine. He had terminal melanoma. Eventually, he just up and disappeared. No notice. No conversation. No explanation. *Okay, mister dark and handsome, be free, fly away, and do your own thing.* And he did just that. He had been somewhat of an independent, free spirit in the past, but he always returned—until he didn't.

When his time came to die, he went back to the shelter of his family and his maker. And he didn't say goodbye. I let him go. *Be free my love, be free.*

Why did this man of honor and integrity shut me out of his life in his last days and exclude me from his departing journey? That is something on which I can only speculate. Was it a matter of courage? Or was it selfishness? No doubt our relationship would have complicated the situation with his family who became his caretakers. He knew I would not be able to let go of *us* easily, and he wanted me to remember him as he was—strong and proud. He would have wanted to spare me the torment of seeing him sick and fading. I would have cried and cried, potentially taking away from his reservoir of strength. I could never have said goodbye. He knew that. Still...I wondered.

Well, I did cry and cry. I sat at his funeral at a prominent African American church in north Tulsa and could not stop crying. An elderly woman took me in, pulled me close to her, put her arm around me and said, "You were his love, weren't you?" And I cried some more as I nodded while tears streamed down my face. She knew. She comforted me as I melted into her arms. "Thank you," I said. Thank you was not enough for what she did for me that day. I will not forget the comfort of a stranger, one who helped me believe people of different races can come together. We can overcome. Yes, we can.

My heart was sad for my love because I knew he did what he had to do in the end, and it was a tough call for him. I believe he could not fix the situation and his abandoning me was not what he wanted to do. It was what he had to do. Not everything can be fixed. His health demanded he be cared for by his family. There were no good answers—no solution.

I understood the denial of our relationship, but it still hurt, and I'm sure it hurt him as well. It would have been too much for me to bear and continue with my work demands. He would have wanted me to go on, so he ended our relationship by leaving. On our last time together, he looked into my eyes and told me I was a woman of destiny. As I look back, I know he knew of his fate at that time but didn't want to reveal it to me.

His final gift to me was to forbid me to see his decline. I have concluded that his intention was to spare each of us a painful goodbye and to avoid the complications of introducing our relationship into his family in his final days. As days went by my heart was sick. I was unable to focus on work. I was broken. Even the lovely, tender memories were painful—the loss unbearable.

How lucky was I to have had such a great love for so long—thirteen splendid years. I live to make him proud and to share his messages: help people realize their potential, act with integrity, be humble, be generous, and be kind.

If I had known when it was the last time I would see his face or nestle into his embrace, I would have held him tighter. I would have made him the best-fried chicken ever and kissed him for longer than thirty minutes. And I would have prayed more.

Kian, a pillar in the community, a business leader, a nobleman of power and honor impacted countless lives. Bestowed with numerous honors and awards, he was a proud man, but there wasn't an ounce of arrogance in him. With a heart for serving others, he led a life of service. At his funeral, a prominent person in the legal community stated, "He was one of the finest who wore the robe." He made the world a better place.

Kian died eight years ago. I put off writing this memoir for many reasons, and he was one of the main ones. To relive the pain and grief seemed too much to bear.

Will I forever mourn and spend my life in sorrow? Will I die of a broken heart? Or will I rally, as I have done many times before, find meaning in this loss and discover a new way forward? Where to, what now? After Kian left and the word of his illness and early retirement were made public, which I observed from afar, I received a phone call that further changed the trajectory of my life...a summons from my mother.

My Dearest Kian

You were a noble and decent man in every sense of these words—a
man worth knowing. A man worth loving. The memories we shared are
captured forever in my heart because we had a forever love, one not broken
by the color of our skin or the end of our time together.

Our love is not broken by the opinions of others or the fractures
of their minds
It is not broken by death
It is not broken by tears that fell—and still do
Our love lives, woven into my heart where it is safe. It comforts me.
Your work here is done. Mine remains. I will make it count as you did.

I measure my life by the stars in the sky, not by the tears that fall
In Heaven there is no ethnicity, race, or religious divide
Only pure love remains
Our love was the melding of two souls with a fire that will never die
Ours is a forever love

Joan Sandergard

————————————

*There is a field. I will meet you there...*Rumi

CHAPTER 19

I'VE BEEN MOM-ED

MOM SAVED ME, AND I BECAME THE BEST OF HER

"Travel light," Mom said. It was June 2015, when exhausted from extensive work hours and mourning over the loss of love, I boarded a plane in Tulsa bound to JFK airport in New York. There I would meet up with my eighty-three-year-old mother who was flying in from California where she lived. We were traveling to Paris.

I struggled with my decision to accompany Mom there because of my emotional state, but I hoped the distraction would help me heal from a loss that had left me unanchored. I needed to go. Still, it was not an easy choice. How could I choose between going and staying back with my dying beloved? This question was answered for me. At that point, Kian had shut me out of his life as his illness progressed, and I had no contact with him. And there was no indication that would change. I was certain he didn't want me to see him in that state. My elderly mother had summoned me, and the decision was made. I chose to go with her to Europe.

I wanted to bring Mom joy as she was restless and eager to travel. So, I went to Europe for her as much as for myself. I was desperate for a distraction, and her for an adventure. And, of course, she was determined to save me. Although my body was drained and my mind cloudy, I put on my comfy big girl stretch pants, stuffed plenty of tissue into my purse, packed my bag, and met Mom in New York. I spotted her as someone wheeled her to our departing gate. Her eyes twinkled and a broad, toothy grin crossed her face when she spotted me. She lunged back and forth trying to get the airport wheelchair pusher to go faster. The sight of her warmed and comforted me. My mom, my rock. I needed her more than ever.

What a time that was—a time of grief beyond measure. As it turned out, I would endure the final loss, the death of my love, while in Paris—the city of love. As the news traveled, I stumbled across the notice of his passing as I glanced at my cell phone. The gut-wrenching news invoked a mental and physical reaction. I ached. It was as though I had been stabbed in the heart. I cried, I cried, and I cried some more. Would my tears forever flow?

I managed to carry on for the rest of the trip despite the burden of agonizing sorrow. Part of my motivation for doing so was for Mom's sake. I needed to rescue her as much as he needed to rescue me. My mother, a saint, once again saw my heart raw and bleeding from a loss. She had gone through the loss of my young husband with me years ago. Years later, I noted an entry in her journal in which she described that time as the most painful, excruciating experience she had ever gone through. No doubt it was painful for her to again see me in that deep state of grief. Solid and one to shoulder troubling times internally, Mom was a rock, but I knew she ached for me. It was comforting to be with her at that time of torment. Even though outwardly she rarely expressed emotion, I sensed that observing my grief was difficult for her.

Because of her upbringing and the reserved nature of Iowans, Mom was a pragmatic realist and a private person not prone to emotional expressions. The westward migration of immigrants introduced into middle America were people highly influenced by a rigid Northern European culture in which people were task-oriented and rarely expressive of emotions. Mom fit solidly into this category. Her motto was:" Head up, be strong, and carry on." Even with her limited height and small, bird-like frame, I would describe her as sturdy. In times of trouble, her calm, stoic nature was just what I needed.

An avid world traveler, she was the perfect travel guide. I relished the memories of that trip. Our time in Paris included a boat ride down the Seine River—a beautiful scenic cruise she had made several times over the years. After Paris, we toured Strasburg, Trier, Koblenz, and Frankfurt, where a breathtaking cruise on the Rhine River delighted us. Like stepping back in time, the gift of travel, on which mom was an expert, soothed me. It was as though I had my very own private, expert tour guide.

Mom's strength and endurance were unusual for someone eighty-three years of age. To embark on such a journey in spite of her limitations was courageous—driven by her love for travel and desire to see the world. Some of the physical challenges were too much for her, but she took in all she could and enjoyed every moment. An ardent observer, she entertained herself by gazing at the sights and watching people as I meandered around. She waited patiently at a sidewalk café or on a park bench, unable to make some of the climbs or walks. As I approached her afterward, her eyes shone and sparkled the second she caught sight of me returning. Although Mom suffered with me over my loss, she no doubt experienced comfort from affording me the gift of our trip together.

We dined on the Rhine with a gentleman who asked us to be guests at his table. We lingered with Fritz over dinner and wine. He was quick to be helpful to Mom as he escorted us to a couple of sites she had inquired about during dinner. He eventually amused me with an invitation to join him and move to Boppard, Germany. He offered everything short of a proposal. An alluring charmer, Fritz loved flirting and was generous with compliments for both Mom and me. His smile and eyes were engaging and his company delightful. Mom relished drinking beer with him and enjoyed his conversation; nevertheless, she was relieved when I refused his proposal. As for me, it was nice to know that "I've still got *it*, whatever *it* is," especially after my recent loss.

Our trip together was everything and more. As I look back now, I see how the stars aligned to protect me. Paris diverted my thoughts and isolated me from public chatter, news articles, and photos flooding the papers and other media reports back home. My love was well-known in the community and people where I worked knew about our relationship. Contact with them would have made it difficult for me to maintain my composure. I could not bear the thought of sympathetic attention. Also, lonely nights at home had become unbearable. The distraction of Mom and Europe was what I needed, and I plodded determinedly through her agenda.

After two weeks of European experiences, it was time to say goodbye to Mom and depart the fabulous continent of Europe. What a blessing it was for me to have had that time with her and to experience her maternal nurturing of my mind and spirit as well as for her to have had that final, splendid trip. I was so proud of Mom—a spunky, fascinating woman who lived life fearlessly and to the fullest. Her story is enduring, empowering and rich with strength, grit, and resiliency. She lived in a way that inspired hope in others, as she did during that difficult time in my life.

And so, it was that I would arrive back home just in time to attend Kian's funeral.

***

Mom loved people, and she was always interested in everyone she met. She was intelligent, a lifelong learner, and a conversationalist extraordinaire. She possessed an amazing memory. Fascinated by people, she remembered details of the lives of every person she met. Mom believed she could do anything she wanted. She always found a way to put her goals into action and live life her way. A top-notch, determined negotiator, she didn't take no for an answer. Energetic, bold, and strong, Mom possessed an adventurous spirit. And there was never any doubt but that she was "in charge."

Born in 1932 at home in Goldfield, Iowa, Mom married my father at the age of twenty-one. After graduating from Simpson College in Indianola, Iowa, she taught fifth grade in Correctionville, Iowa. She was married to my father for forty years, and they had five children, seven grandchildren, and four great-grandchildren.

Mom was a member of Pi Beta Phi sorority, St Pius Catholic Church, and other organizations throughout her life, including twenty-six years in Parent Teacher Associations. Family, friends, church, education, health, and travel were important to her. She was resourceful and mentally and physically strong, though she usually carried less than ninety-five pounds of weight on her five-foot-three frame. Her faith in God was steadfast, and she looked forward to Mass wherever she might be.

Mom, a homemaker, approached her forties with her five children growing up and a new vision in sight. She became determined to make her dreams of traveling to Europe come true. With expenses required to raise so many children and her husband, a pharmacist with limited income, she knew the finances were not there to fulfill her dream. What could she do? How could she make that happen? Obstacles never stopped Mom. They only made her more determined to find a solution. Her resourcefulness, skills, and tenacity kicked in. Mom was going to Europe.

She planned, set a goal, and established a time frame. Two of my sisters wanted to go to Europe with her. So, she recruited them to help collect bottles, newspapers, and cans for recycling. She was incredibly frugal and accumulated money in a jar as she educated herself on her travel dreams. She accomplished her goal at the age of forty-seven and traveled to Europe for the first of thirty-six times and visited twenty-one European countries throughout her life. She did so economically with her motto: travel light and cheap. She was a *diva on a dime.*

Dad, who had no desire to travel, supported Mom's pursuit of travel goals. I admired him for his self-confidence and willingness to let her follow her dreams. He enjoyed watching her soar as she made her journeys.

Dad passed away in 1993, and Mom moved to California in 1996 to be near my sister. She left behind thirty years of friends, her home, Iowa roots, and midwestern life to brave a new world with my sister who agreed to care for her in her aging years. The Iowa winters, life without Dad, and the need to pursue a new chapter in her life inspired her to forge ahead with courage and anticipation. It was there that she found love again at the age of sixty-eight with a man eight years her junior.

Mom dismantled her three-story home by herself, downsized, and moved into a six-hundred-square-foot high-rise apartment in Huntington Beach, California. Unlike most older people, material things didn't matter to her, and she let go of material possessions easily. Her mental toughness kicked in and she embraced minimalism as she forged ahead with the task of downsizing and starting over in California. With parents who went through the depression, she learned to be resourceful and thrifty, and she was appreciative of the smallest of life's comforts. What mattered most to Mom was life's experiences, which included seeing the world, and helping others achieve their full potential.

After Mom moved to California, far from her homeland and thirty years of rooted friendships, she became lonely. My sister worked many hours and, although Mom was involved in her grandchildren's activities, there was a void in her life. She enjoyed walking to the Huntington Beach pier, often stopping at McDonald's for a cup of coffee or a bite to eat.

With her friendly nature, she greeted the locals wherever she went. One day at McDonald's, she observed a gentleman sitting at a table by himself enjoying a cup of coffee and introduced herself. They chatted briefly. Two weeks later at McDonald's, the same gentleman sat there by himself reading a newspaper. This time, after engaging in conversation, she asked him out on a date. He accepted. What began as a simple greeting ended up as a courtship and a love story. My mother remarried at the age of seventy. Excited and as happy as high schoolers in love, they traveled the world together.

In 2008, she traveled to Budapest by herself at the age of seventy-six where she spent the summer alone in the thermal healing waters. She researched medical insurance policies to identify spas to treat her rheumatoid arthritis, a condition she learned to defeat every day. In 2012, at the age of eighty, Mom decided she wanted to go to Albania, Tirana, and Saranda. And she did. After sending out an email to her children with no advance notice and an unknown return date, off she went. "Tattoo your home address on your body," I told her, "So they will know where to send you."

She disregarded anyone trying to discourage her or discredit her abilities. Shrugging off any worries her family expressed about her life or travels, she said, "If I don't pay my rent, they will come looking for me." Making friends was not a problem for Mom, as she took a great interest in everyone she met during her travels, often leaving them with a compliment regarding their spoken English, education, vocation, or whatever pleased her. She made it a practice to make friends with the priests as she rolled into towns, which I'm certain contributed to her fearless nature. She made certain they had her back, and that Jesus was on her side.

***

Things took a turn after Mom returned from our trip to Europe. She continued to experience pain from a back condition that had plagued her for years and decided to pursue surgery. This was a tremendous undertaking for her age and ninety-pound frame. She had never been under anesthesia in her life. She shopped around and found a surgeon who would operate and successfully went through surgery. Courageously, she completed rehabilitation. During this time, I went back and forth to California to help her during her recuperation process. She surprised everyone, including the surgeon, with a quicker-than-expected recovery.

A few months later, Mom was back to her usual routine, walking daily to the pier and doing well. But soon thereafter, on December 18, 2016, I got a call at work. She had suffered a brain aneurysm and was on life support in the hospital. This was six months after my boyfriend died. I boarded a plane to join my siblings at the hospital where we would honor her wishes and remove her from life support. Her heart stopped while I was in flight. Mom traveled to the great unknown on December 19, 2016. I didn't get to say goodbye. In a sense, that was a blessing, and perhaps she knew that. I would have been horrified seeing her hooked up to machines in a vegetative state. She did it her way, just as she lived her life. She Mom-ed me one last time.

Over the years, Mom and I talked almost daily. With that contact gone and the ongoing anguish I experienced from the loss of Kian, I was crushed with pain and heartache. But I learned a valuable lesson. When you think you can't take anymore, you can.

After her unexpected death, with intense grief and an inconsolable ache in my heart, I reminded myself that she would want me to be strong and carry on each day. I comforted myself with memories, especially of our bonding travel adventurers. I accompanied her as often as possible over the years. Together we went to Europe four times in addition to St. Martin and Mexico. I'll never forget when we came upon a nude beach. "Quick, Mom, close your eyes," I said. Not only did she not close her eyes; after staring gleefully at a young, buck-naked man on a jet ski, she stripped off her swimsuit and walked into the sea. I laughed until I couldn't laugh anymore. Nor will I forget my first trip with her to Europe to celebrate my fortieth birthday in Vienna, Austria. Mom said I could bring one rolling carry-on bag. "For three weeks?" I asked. Not knowing how I could fit clothes, shoes, makeup, and hair items into one roll-on suitcase, I agreed to do it her way and asked her for a packing list. As was often the case, she was right. Traveling light was the best.

Through the seasons of my life, Mom was there, helping me through the tears, and disarming every dart life threw at me. During my early years, she let me down in a sense when she did not acknowledge the reality of the molestation. But knowing the Iowa culture and women of that generation, I realize how intensely difficult it was for her to face the truth of what her husband had done. Her response was incredibly normal for her time. As always, her approach was to buck up and carry on past the issue. Mom eventually rallied to my side and became my most enthusiastic champion. Strong, devoted, and relentless, she taught me the importance of living in the now—*to just be*. I also learned from her to stay the course and redeem yourself when you mess up in life. Mom knew how to rebound from a crisis.

Many times, throughout my life, I've been Mom-ed. She often said, "Take the adventure and enjoy the journey." Mom defined difficult events as "life happening." The journey of recovering from lost love and my loss of her was a long, arduous road that called for a determined, intentional rally. So, I braced myself and carried on throughout a healing process rich with peaks and valleys. And I did so, as Mom would have wanted, with bravado and the willful determination *to just be.*

Life happened, and Mom was gone. I spent a good part of my younger years trying not to be like her. Now, as a well-seasoned woman, I realized how much I was like her and what a blessing that was because I became the best of her. Let's face it, I've been royally and thoroughly Mom-ed.

To My Angel Mother

As the ocean hurls waves onto the shore and the sun warms my wrinkling skin, a seagull makes its way in the light of day and the tide ebbs. Another day is born, and I think of you.

Your journey was met with adversity and hardship. Courageous and strong, you refused to let go, fiercely protecting me, holding my hand until I was nurtured back, and trust was restored.

You set me free, healed and rejuvenated and no longer a captive to this world. And so, the life cycle carries on. Your legacy of moxie and adventurous spirit lives in me.

I was young and now I am old. My body tires as I contemplate all you gave to me. My mother, my rock, my everything, all I was, am, or hope to be I owe to you, my angel mother.

You are the flowers on the windowsill, the sun that warms my back, and the beckoning that calls me home. It's the call of love, and someday, hand in hand, I will eagerly go.

Joan Sandergard

CHAPTER 20

LOVE HURTS-HEARTS HEAL

SOME LOVES ARE TRANSIENT. BETRAYAL, THOUGH, IS ENDURING

Betrayal burns like embers refusing to extinguish until nothing, but ashes remain. Lost love fosters a deep, gnawing pain with memories that refuse to wither. From love and loss experiences, I learned the profound lesson of hope I had embraced when Mom died: *When I think I can't take any more hurt, I can.* That doesn't mean the road to healing was easy. It was not. Doing so required forgiveness, and a deep analysis of the why's behind human behavior.

Betrayal can take many forms, and in my life, it did. A combination of a sense of abandonment and disillusionment pulled me into its snare several times, trapping me and introducing a cruel path to persistent emotional turmoil rooted in heartache. My dad, my husband, and my boyfriend of thirteen years, let me down in different but excruciating ways. Those losses impacted my ability to trust and accept love, leaving me to shut out feelings. I wanted a forever love but found it unattainable. For years, I associated it with pain and loss, which kept serious relationships at bay.

***

Dad's betrayal of my innocence took away the fatherly love from my childhood. I didn't feel protected by my parents. Anger, insecurity, and a nagging feeling that what happened was my fault caused me to rebel as a teenager. The loss of trust in those who should have protected me left me unanchored. I was not okay and felt as though I could not rely on the guidance and direction of my parents. This caused me to self-protect, to run away, and to find my own way without direction. Fear and hurt took over, impacting every fiber of my being. My self-esteem suffered setting off the innate fighting spirit in me that drove me to rebellion. I and my entire family paid a heavy price for that choice.

The consequences of those childhood experiences caused me to impulsively initiate several fixes that made things worse. I eventually found my footing and figured out how to rally successfully. I was near thirty when I did so, and undoubtedly, much of this progress was the result of an internal motivation—an inherent belief in myself, a determined fighting spirit, and the desire to protect my daughter.

My husband, my first and greatest romantic love, left suddenly in a tragic, heartless way, which was a betrayal of our love and commitment. He had his reasons. He was a hurt child, but so was I. Eventually, I understood where his flawed reasoning originated. But still, what he did stabbed my heart. His action destroyed my dream of a forever love and left me wondering. *Could I survive another loss? Could I, would I love again?*

Bodie killed himself according to a coroner, but I blamed myself and shouldered considerable guilt, which was a heavy burden for a teenager or anyone to bear. I floundered initially but ultimately rallied. As a vulnerable young widow and mother, I fought against all odds for something better for years after his death.

Eventually, I buried the stigma, guilt, and pain of spousal suicide. I was not the culprit. Bodie, as an adult, had choices, and he made a miserable one that day. I came to accept that only God knows his intent and what was in his heart. I've let him go, to be free, the free bird he always wanted to be. Today I seek to live my life to the fullest for him, for his daughter, and for others who might suffer as he did.

Many years would pass before I could again open my heart to love. And when it did, as wondrous as it was, that love flung me into an abyss. When Kian shut me out of his life, he had his reasons, but his doing so left me disillusioned and his actions made me wonder if he cared for me at all. I questioned whether his love was real. To me it was a great love and worth the hurt, but that did nothing to mitigate the pain his abandonment provoked.

Recognizing the cultural and ethnic divide that complicated and influenced his behavior in the end, I have moved beyond the pain. Although I didn't understand initially why he chose not to say goodbye, it was a betrayal. Now I understand the reasons behind the sacrifice he made. His options were limited. The one he made, he made for me.

These three losses scarred me. For years I harbored an intense distrust of the prospect that love would last. I associated it with trauma, struggle, dependency, and hurt. Independence set in, and I sought no heroes to rescue me. I needed to heal and to stand on my own.

***

Lost love, especially when combined with betrayal is a sucker punch. Damage from it cuts deep. At certain points, I struggled to live. At times I hurt so much inside from these experiences that I felt as though someone had ripped open my stomach and tore my guts out, leaving a gaping hole and dangling, bleeding tentacles. The constant grinding hurt was so intense it occasionally brought me just short of the grave. I would do *almost* anything to make it stop. This description may sound overly dramatic, but the potency of the torment I internalized, especially in those younger years, cannot be overstated. Angel was my reason to carry on and without her, I may not have done so.

I was tossed into the sea as the storms hurled me farther into the depths of a dark, murky ocean. When would the toll of betrayal become too much to bear, and love would no longer be an option? Not yet. My heart and mind remained open to the prospect. Although scars remained from the devastating sting of these losses, healing came when I realized the medicine was mine. It was up to me to heal myself.

I learned that people who were hurt, hurt people. Why? Because people were flawed, and addiction, mental illness, disease, harsh backgrounds, and socio-economic factors influenced actions that—whether intentional or not—hurt people. Society, religion, politics, and institutions sometimes hurt people. Greed and selfish ambitions hurt people. Powerful words hurt people. Though most often unintended, ignorance and misunderstandings hurt people. As a measure of self-defense, frightened and wounded people abuse others. Abandonment, laced with betrayal, hurts people.

Being a parent was the catalyst that caused me to fight through the hurt and heal from all those experiences. To go beyond them to live a purposeful life through a rewarding career was a bonus. I leaned into what many would have considered unsurmountable challenges and learned I could do hard things. I went from being a confused, wounded, angry, defiant teenager to an independent woman who had influence—who mattered.

Guided by a greater sense of self, I was no longer a victim of circumstances. As a single mom, I overcame my past and raised an exceptionally talented, and successful daughter. Resilient in every way, she did everything right growing up. Unlike her mother, she avoided a stage of rebellion and poor judgment during her youth and matured into a gracious, kind adult with a giving heart. A Southern Methodist University graduate, she demonstrated good judgment by marrying a wonderful man, and she became the best mother ever. Strong and capable, she would easily be a testament to overcoming being raised without a father and by a young, single mom who floundered in her early years. After a rough start, together we believed and overcame. We were a team.

Forgiveness came when I understood that we were all a result of our childhood and life experiences. For me, that realization introduced compassion, understanding, and healing. I had a choice to forgive others—and myself—or to carry the weight of bitterness. I was unable to experience the concept of mutual forgiveness in person with Bodie or Kian, but I did in the matter of my father.

***

It was 1991 when Dad traveled to Tulsa where I lived. I was in my thirties. I suspected he had a premonition that his health was failing. Although I had forgiven him years ago for his unfortunate behavior, we further reconciled our relationship. We enjoyed laughs and hugs, toured around town, ate raw oysters, and had a wonderful time together. Shortly after he returned to Iowa, he was diagnosed with incurable lung cancer at the age of sixty. He was a smoker, and the habit took its toll.

Dad was given a year to live. Having an exceptionally strong work ethic, he had never taken a sick day off work in his life, and he worked up to his final days. He didn't once complain when his chest was burned with radiation. The cancer spread, but he continued to work.

During his last year, Angel and I made several road trips to Iowa. We celebrated his and Mom's fortieth wedding anniversary with friends and family. We told stories, shared hugs, and laughed. One of the highlights of Dad's life was when he traveled to Denmark to meet the family on his biological father's side. Their long-lost son had come home, and they put on a celebratory feast. "It was like killing the fatted calf," he said, as they lifted their glasses to toast." Dad spoke with joy in his final days about his Danish family. His life came full circle. He had come home.

Mom became Dad's caretaker. They developed a new appreciation for each other and found peace and happiness in their relationship at last. However, Dad refused to take time off work. He worked and thrived that last year—doing what he loved—working with employees and serving customers. Mom accepted that. As his disease progressed, hospice was called to the home. Dad stopped working. His heart stopped two days later.

"Come home to say goodbye. It won't be long," Mom said to me. His death was imminent. As I sat on a plane ready to take flight, an overhead announcement in the cabin called me to the front of the plane. It was an emergency call from my mother. She had managed to get through to the right person to stop the plane from taking off so she could talk on the phone to me. *Oh, My Lord. How did she do that, and why?* Mom was resourceful and had a way of making anything happen. No one said "no" to Mom. She told me Dad had passed away, and that I may not want to come yet, but that he was "there waiting for me." *This makes no sense. Okay. He is waiting for me, dead?* It was not unusual for Mom to leave me scratching my head after some illogical comment. I continued my flight to Iowa sobbing so much that they put me on the last row of the plane with a box of Kleenex.

Dad couldn't wait for me to say goodbye. I was a Daddy's girl, deeply wounded by this loss and struggling with a complicated grief. I sobbed for weeks. My heart felt like someone had taken an enormous chunk out of it. With tears rolling down my eyes, I played the flute at his funeral, as he requested— *The Lord's Prayer* put in song format. It was the sound of peace. Dad was at peace, and I was grateful for that.

Mom, who was Catholic, had called a priest to the home shortly before he died. Dad was highly intelligent and a rational, critical thinker. He questioned information presented in the Bible, often with his self-researched evidence. He questioned faith and religion in general and in its various forms. He questioned pastors who had no answers that made sense to him. And he asked me questions when I was in theology school, and I had no answers. No doubt, Dad didn't embrace Catholicism on his deathbed, but I suspect he reconciled his faith and found peace with his perception of spirituality and his God in the end.

I am grateful for the foundation Dad built for me in my younger years: the strong work ethic, the fortitude to fight, and the perseverance to get back up and continue no matter what. Sober, clean, independent, strong, and beginning my career, I was in a good place when he died. But his death took its toll. I couldn't sleep and was put on medication for a few months until I could function without it. I took comfort in the fact that he was not suffering anymore and eventually stopped feeling sorry for myself over the loss. It was hard on my body to carry the grief. Mourning could not bring him back. It was time to let go.

Grief was like traveling through a deep dark tunnel I had to go through on my own. Nothing—absolutely nothing—not alcohol, drugs, food, new relationships, geographical changes, or tears—could make it disappear. I steeled myself by going inward to let the pain wear itself out so I could surface with renewed strength. I learned that grief had its own timeline, and it could make or break a person. And I knew my loved ones lived in my heart and would always be a part of me. Dad made one mistake. We all make mistakes and who knows what he went through in the orphanage without his mother or as a child. I chose to forgive him years ago, and we both overcame that unfortunate time in our lives. It is important to note that he was a good man. He invested in me, and after he died, I grasped a newfound purpose—to live in a way that would make him proud and that would give him a return on his investment.

My siblings and I put tennis shoes on Dad's feet as he was dressed in a tailored suit for viewing. He had a sense of humor and would have loved that. I've thought of Dad often with gratitude for the accountability, maturity, and forgiveness that brought us back together before he was gone.

I had been in and out of love all my life. Some loves faded. Others were forever. My love for Dad was a forever love.

"Love comes to those who still
hope after disappointment,
who still believe after
betrayal, and who still love
after they've been hurt."

Anonymous

CHAPTER 21

MATTERING AND LEAVING IT BETTER

LEGACY THE MOTIVATION—A FLUTE THE MEDICINE

A s a sixty-something woman with years of lessons learned, I found myself thinking about things that I never considered during my younger years. One of those things for me was creating legacy. I wanted to make a difference—which meant being purposeful. Someone asked June Carter Cash one day how she was doing. She responded, "I'm just trying to matter." It occurred to me that this was where I was. Having rallied from the turmoil of the early years and then successfully raising an amazing daughter, and ultimately retiring from a meaningful career, I now focused on continuing to make my life matter. Part of this mission was to create a legacy. Writing this memoir was a way to do that.

Memoir writing required a life review. Looking back, it was clear my life was teemed with significant ups and downs. When trying to fix a problem, I sometimes failed and made things worse. But I didn't quit. I stayed in the ring. The early years of floundering left me dirty and marred. However, no matter what was thrown my way or how unanchored I felt, giving up was not an option. With a fierce motivation to overcome, I ultimately became a winner, at the top of my game. A desire to finish strong and to believe in myself and others persisted throughout the years, and that same determination continued to influence my future now.

George Bernard Shaw said, *"A life spent making mistakes is not only more honorable, but more useful than a life spent doing nothing."*

My younger years as a promised child were tarnished by sexual abuse and the poor decisions that followed. I missed out on a lot because of that, but I wasn't going to miss out on being a mother. And although I struggled with that role initially, I rallied from whatever challenge stood in the way. I survived—which in and of itself was astounding.

Ultimately, in my late twenties, I summoned the strength and fortitude to be the mother my daughter deserved. And I was in my thirties when finally, the morning came—the dawn of a new day when I discovered a sense of purpose by helping others through my career. In my forties, I found love and joy. In my sixties, I wrote this book believing I am on the cusp of mattering even more.

Once I found my lane in a career that allowed me to make a difference in the lives of others, I tapped into the unfortunate experiences of those early years and used them to inspire. Those missteps promoted a sense of compassion for others that I would not have had otherwise. I invited people to walk with me, to overcome, to never give up, to believe in themselves, to have hope, and to know that there was a better way.

Life experiences taught me so much. Through those experiences, I discovered a gift. Deep within me was a warrior. My past prepared me for work with adolescents, Domestic Violence Intervention Services, and the State Department of Human Services. I had the perspective of someone who had been through turmoil, and I saw families and their situations through a lens that those who lived more cushioned lives could not. I was particularly compassionate when it came to single mothers. I had walked that walk. I believed in teenage mothers and was perhaps more understanding and lenient with them than others would have been. In addition, I had experienced addiction and sexual abuse. And my life had been impacted by the domestic violence my husband witnessed as a child. Because of those experiences, I was able to empower others to reach out for help and to believe they could recover.

Throughout my adult life, I embraced continuous learning and knew the value of credentials, both of which supported my rally. Extensive professional training throughout my career in multiple areas equipped me to not only be empathetic with the downtrodden, but to advise them wisely. I know one person can make a difference because I did so, many times over—and I aspire to continue to do so.

I have played many roles during my lifetime: a mother, daughter, granddaughter, sister, Grandma Gigi, niece, cousin, aunt, and great aunt, but the role I'm most proud of is being a mother. As I look back on the accomplishments and milestones in my life, my greatest achievement stands out—raising my daughter. I made mistakes, as all parents do, but like most, I did the best I could with what I had, what I knew, and the situations that confronted me. The naivety of youth attributed to a lot of the unfortunate behavior I exhibited as a young mother in my teens and early twenties. A friend of mine summed up that notion when she said, "When you are that young, you don't know what you don't know." There was so much I didn't know.

Although I was young and damaged when I became a mother, I finished strong. The outcome speaks for itself. Angel—sweet angel. Through good times and challenging ones, she was my motivation—a reason to live, to never give up, and to get back up after failure, to believe in a brighter tomorrow, and to fight for a better way. I wanted the best for her, so when traumas jeopardized that, I fought to overcome and be the best I could be. I worked hard for healing, recovery, and self-growth.

I raised Angel on my own for seventeen years with little help. Although I dated occasionally, I avoided a serious relationship until she was grown and on her own. I recognized the risk of trauma or hurt bringing another person into the home could cause.

Angel was my joy, my love, my everything. As a young girl, she excelled in voice and piano as well as tennis and ice skating. A strong swimmer, she became an instructor and lifeguard. At an early age, she developed an independent nature and an adventurous spirit. And she ultimately blossomed into a remarkable woman, wife, and mother.

Her teenage years were hard, in the normal way. With the introduction of hormones and the process of seeking independence, she began her journey to leave the nest. It was difficult for me when she went away to college, but my tears were balanced with a sense of pride for the person she had become. For years, it had been her and me, and the agonizing loss of that intimate connection cut deep. It ushered me into another phase of my life.

I learned to be strong, and happy. The Dalai Lama said in his book, *The Art of Happiness*, "If you want to be happy, practice compassion." I have lived that message.

I also grew to bask in gratefulness. I was forever grateful to my family members who didn't stop believing in me and loving me when I was a hot mess, especially my mother. She rescued me and my daughter and forgave me for the occasions I failed. I have missed Mom every day since she died, but her lessons have also influenced me each day. I am determined to live in a way that would make her proud. She invested in me—saved me actually—and, like Dad, I owe her a return on that investment.

Making peace with God sustained my faith. He took my hand and gently led me out of darkness, and I am thankful to the many angels along my journey. I have been blessed with the gift of spirituality and heartfelt compassion. This perspective provided a roadmap for a purposeful life.

I was blessed with many friends over the years. They didn't judge me but walked with me through what seemed like endless ordeals. Several mentors have guided me along the way as well. Because of these supporters, I chose to pay it forward.

When I was younger, I believed I could fix anything if I tried hard enough. However, I found that sometimes I had to surrender and choose another path after giving it my best shot. I did not view myself as a victim and wore my sufferings and stories of destruction proudly as a badge of honor. In the end, I was a winner. I aspired to reach higher, to overcome and be better, to matter, and to make a difference in any small way I could.

I was fortunate to have had music as my medicine—my path to healing, and my passion. I played the piano, the piccolo, guitar, and sang vocals, but through it all, it was the sound of the flute that carried me through. The talent for playing it was innate—what I was born to do. This powerful, unique gift became a source of healing when I needed it most. During my darkest days when menacing clouds hovered, I shut down and abandoned playing because doing something joyful was contrary to my desolate mood. Eventually, though, I discovered that the medicine was mine and the flute was a tool to be used on the path to recovery. I carried it all over the country for fifty-some years. It was a reminder of who I was, that I was somebody. When I lost myself, I found comfort and peace in music.

As a child, I wanted to play the harp. Mom encouraged me to play the flute. She prevailed and saved me from lugging a harp around throughout my life. I easily tucked my flute case away in a piece of luggage, loaded it into a car, or stored it in a closet. She pushed me to practice and taught me discipline. Wanting me to be the best I could be, she insisted I not settle for mediocrity, and she encouraged the practice required to excel. I was Mom-ed.

Throughout most of my life, I played. I performed in youth symphonies, orchestras, bands, on worship teams, in churches, nursing homes, retirement communities, and at weddings, funerals, and other places and events. I taught flute lessons and took lessons for years. Because of my musical background, I often woke up in the middle of the night and went to the piano to compose songs.

My flute and I were one. I clung to it as if it were a life vest on a drowning woman, and at times it was. My flute was there when I couldn't fix the storms raging around me, particularly in the early years when I was free falling. When fixes made things worse, I bolted—with my flute. My flute was a source of comfort and the channel through which my voice could be heard, and my essence expressed. It made room for me. The flute was a blessing—the one consistent thing that was mine, a part of me that no one could take away.

Through the early life experiences, I learned the importance of holding myself accountable, to be a warrior rather than a victim, to become my own advocate. I learned to fail better when I couldn't win. I was dependent and later became independent and resilient. Although once weak, I built emotional strength. I realized I would be happy because I had known great sorrow. Mistakes produced wisdom. I forgave because I had been forgiven. I became brave because of my scars. I won because I never quit. And I loved because I was loved.

Recently, I chose a new love—writing. Writing completed me. When I wrote, time passed, and I didn't realize it. I didn't feel as though I should be doing something else. Like playing the flute, writing made me feel as though I was doing what I was born to do.

Writing my memoir created fresh perspectives on my past, which helped me explore choices as I looked toward the final years of my life. I've been told that memoirs create legacy. My first book was this memoir. There will be more, but I started here because I wanted legacy to serve as a gift, and I am determined to tell my story and share my hard-earned wisdom.

When I think back on my life, I realize that, unfortunately, I never experienced a good goodbye when those I cared most about died. In fact, I didn't get a goodbye at all. They just up and went away. I had no closure with my husband, my father, my love, and my mother. I don't know what it's like to say goodbye or to share last words before someone dies. The shock of my husband's suicide and the abrupt end of my love of many years left me tortured and unanchored. With my parents I tried to be present as they slipped away, but they both passed when I was on a plane. Those losses without goodbyes left a mark. If I had known it was going to be the last time I would see their faces, what would I have said? What would I have done? Would I have crawled into bed beside them, snuggled in, and held on tight? Probably.

I will create my destiny. I will love—today and tomorrow—in whatever form that takes. When I lie down and close my eyes for the final time, I want to know that my life counted for something—that I mattered, made a difference, and left this world a better place because I was in it. And by doing so, I will know that I experienced a remarkable, exceptional life and left a worthy legacy. I also aspire to experience a good goodbye, not so much for my sake, but for others. I hope I don't die while Angel is on a plane. If someone I love crawls into bed and snuggles with me, I shall relish the moment. If not, that's okay. You can't always get what you want. I got a lot. I had a crazy, wonderful life. It was grand.

Simply grateful, I was just a girl with a flute from Madison County.

To laugh often and much;
To win the respect of intelligent
people and the affection of children;
To earn the appreciation of honest
critics and endure the betrayal of false
friends; To appreciate beauty, to find
the best in others; To leave the world
a bit better, whether by a healthy child,
a garden patch or a redeemed social
condition; To know even one life has
breathed easier because you have lived.
This is to have succeeded.

Ralph Waldo Emerson

EPILOGUE

Lessons Learned

Turn your wounds into wisdom. – Oprah Winfrey

Today, I am in my sixties, and I may have thirty-some years left-one-third of my lifetime. That's a lot of time to waste. I will not coast. I plan to launch again and live purposefully. I will be a beacon of hope, an advocate for change and a champion of people who have no voice. And I will encourage others to join me in those efforts. By doing so, I know that I will continue to live a worthy life.

By being vulnerable and candid about my past, I hope the resulting rally and wisdom will inspire others to aspire, realize positive outcomes, and never give up.

Experience has taught me that one person can make a difference day by day. When I observe an unfortunate situation, I will continue to ask why because that is the path to solutions. Although such an effort might leave a mark on my psyche, just as much of my past work has done, I will stay the course and carry on. And so, I write.

WORTHINESS

Because You Were Born, You Are Worthy

You have nothing to prove. You are unique and special—a gift. Settle into that. Your path, your purpose, your place in the world will come. You will know what that is when time passes while you are doing something, and you don't realize it.

When something bad happens, Grandpa would say, "Keep your chin and lower lip up." Look for the positives—there must be a pony in there somewhere.

Grandpa also used to say, "Stand tall, head up, and shoulders back." Good posture gives you a keen sense of presence when you stand or enter a room. And it suggests quiet confidence, an attribute that can serve you well.

Don't keep track of your mess-ups. Fix them as best you can, let them go, and move on to the next step. Most people judge themselves more harshly than others do. Be easy on yourself, because when you lose or fail, you learn. Surrender can be a positive and productive act. Sometimes we just try too hard.

Avoid comparing yourself to others. Especially, don't measure yourself by those in another age group or in a different set of circumstances. Just be you.

INTEGRITY

Nothing Else Counts if You Don't Have Integrity

Be a person of your word. When you are obligated or committed to do something, do it, *and then some*. When you don't want to do something, do it anyway—*and then some*. It is the *and then some* that will set you apart and pay off big time.

Hold yourself accountable for your role in unfortunate circumstances. When you blame others, you become a victim, which forces someone else into a persecutor role. This promotes unfortunate outcomes for both parties. Blaming others makes you look small. Standing up and taking a hit shows good character.

Taking the high road even when others don't is a matter of integrity. Be the bigger person. Do the right thing.

Walking away from a fight is not weak. It takes more courage to do that than to engage in a confrontation, especially a physical one. If you have a feisty friend eager to fight, warn them that you won't have their back. This is not cowardly. It is good judgment. Physical action is rarely the best option.

Words are powerful. Choose them carefully. You can apologize for unfortunate words, but it is not possible to take them back. They leave scars. If you find yourself often apologizing for your words, change what you say and how you say it, so apologies are not necessary.

Sometimes the truth hurts, but in general, be truthful anyway. There are exceptions, such as when your truth can hurt people with no benefit to them or anyone else.

Don't be careless with your reputation. It is vital that you do not *ever* share anything online that you would not want your parents, or grandparents, other loved ones, potential employers, future mates or their parents, or the world to see. Poor judgment online can haunt you forever. If there is ever a place for dignity and decorum, social media is it.

MAKING A DIFFERENCE

Never Underestimate Your Value to Others

You are always leading. You can never not lead. Everyone leads by how they behave. Be a positive influence—a stand-up person. Aspire to be the voice of reason when people get a bad idea. Be the one who speaks up or questions when others cower. Call out those who mislead or mistreat others. Do so with authority, but never with arrogance.

Take care of people. Be a responder. Make a day better for someone because you are in it. And, if someone passes out at a party or event and partiers stand around drinking and laughing at the fallen person, be the stand-up person who acts and saves them.

Some people coast through life, especially in their senior years. That is not necessarily a bad thing. Avoid judging those who choose to do so. But I wish for you that you don't do that, but instead live your best life full out to the end.

Be a problem solver. Worrying about a problem wastes energy. Focus on doing something about it. Find the root cause and explore viable solutions. Be bold and resourceful at solving problems but know that not every problem is yours to solve nor is every problem one you can solve. Sometimes your role is to determine how to cope with one or to help others do so.

Make people's day all day every day. Assist them. Complement them. Smile at them. Surprise a snippy waitress with a generous tip. Who knows why she was in a bad mood? Perhaps she had no milk for her children that morning or her car broke down. Smile at those who look down and out and be kind to those society generally treats poorly. Rather than saying, "I appreciate *it*," say, "I appreciate *you*."

CONTINUOUS LEARNING

Gandhi said, "Learn as though You Will Live Forever"

Be in a state of continuous learning. When you learn something through reading, study, observation, education, or earning a credential, you are investing in yourself. Knowledge and credentials are things you hold forever. Once achieved, these become a part of you. No one can ever take them away. Invest in yourself through learning.

It is common for young people to be dismissive of the elderly. That is a missed opportunity. An older person can be a prolific source of wisdom and a youngster's biggest champion. Tapping into that gives a person an edge that sets them apart.

Learn from children. Their pristine minds, untarnished by the complicated and cluttered beliefs of adults, offer pure and sensible conclusions.

ENDURANCE

Surviving the Harsh Realities of Life Requires Staying the Course

On your worst days, know that a new day is coming. Something you can say to yourself that keeps you moving forward is: *This, too, will pass.* It will. Nothing stays the same. The universe gives you the gift of a new day—a new start every day. When you are at the bottom, there is no way to go but up. Hold on. Every morning when you awake, be grateful for that day. It is a gift from the universe—one not everyone gets.

Be creative in seeking solutions to problems, but remember, doing nothing is often an okay choice. Endurance melts away many problems. Time is gentle. Time can be your friend. When times are hard, hang in there. *This, too, will pass.*

Life ebbs and flows. Without the bad times, the good ones wouldn't mean much. It's the contrast between the two that makes them relevant. Each exists because of the other. The downs are what make the ups so valued.

No matter what, remember that low points are not forever, and things will get better. The darkest times are temporary. Hang in, keep the faith, stay the course, sit in a cloud, and reach out to loved ones. Never, ever give up on life.

It's a bad idea to use a permanent solution with negative consequences to solve a temporary problem. There are always either alternative solutions or ways to cope. Often, it is just a matter of riding out a situation. The solution is simply time.

It's a sign of a mentally healthy person to seek help when needed. You will have many crises throughout your life. Give yourself a break when you need it and share your feelings with a trusted person. You don't have to shoulder troubles on your own. Reach out.

Often your greatest fear does not materialize or, if it does, it is not as bad as you thought it would be. When you dread something, consider facing it head-on and getting it behind you, so you can look back later and be grateful you endured.

MYTHS
Not All "Words of Wisdom" Are Wise

The statement that "Anything worth doing is worth doing well" is not always true. Sometimes it is better to do something halfway than not at all. A temporary fix may be a better option when a permanent fix is not possible or takes too long.

It is not true that you can be or do anything you want. You can't. Everyone has limitations. Find what you were born to do and do that. Develop your innate gifts and talents. Those attributes are the path to fulfillment and a contented but productive and purposeful life.

Most people think that to relieve stress you need to take a break. However, at times, the best stress reliever is to dig in and get some things off your To-do list.

Some say winners never quit, but at times, walking away may be the best option and the way to win. You can't fix everything. Know when it's time to move on to something else. Sometimes you need to reset your priorities.

Many people believe you must forgive injurious behavior to move in a new direction. Not necessarily. There is no fixed rule on forgiveness. There is no clear formula on what defines it, how to do it, and when it is deserved. You may not be able to forgive—or not want to. That is okay. You can neutralize what happened and find peace by taking it off your agenda. Perhaps some people don't deserve to be forgiven, or maybe you are not healed by giving it. Find your own path.

Some people, especially politicians, suggest that changing your mind is a bad thing. It is not. They label it *wavering*. Hold your beliefs lightly. Wavering can be a good thing when you get new information that supports a change in conclusions. Base your belief system on up-to-date facts. Be open, curious, rational, and flexible. Avoid drawing conclusions from labels, name-calling, rhetoric, or single-source propaganda.

You may train your children on the danger of guns, manage their technology to shut out porn, and educate them on the potential for addiction to gaming or being groomed on TikTok, but all their friends' parents do not do that. It is not uncommon for children to exchange phones. The reality is that your children are at risk for these threats. Your involvement in their lives is essential to counteract these external influences and neutralize their effects. Pay attention.

RELATIONSHIPS
Not Everyone Is Worthy of Your Time
Judge friendships and romantic relationships by how people make you feel. Nothing is as important as that. Judge people by what they do, not what they say. Choose who you run with carefully. You are who you surround yourself with.

Be aware of the behaviors of controlling, and manipulating people. Avoid them. Red flag traits include excessively charismatic and charming, overly dramatic, critical of your family and friends and isolating you from them, building you up and then tearing you down, love bombing (excessive gifts and attention), moving too fast in a relationship, and exhibiting extreme jealousy.

Do not engage with toxic people and avoid people who stir up drama or put you down. Surround yourself with those who champion you and lift you up.

People are flawed. Justifying or defending their mistakes (or yours) encourages bad behavior. Accepting accountability for missteps promotes being a stand-up person. Don't be a patsy and defend wicked or mean people. There are takers and users in the world. Be vigilant and trust your intuition when assessing people and their actions. Again, it is not what people say that counts, it is what they do.

Bullies are persecutors—cowards who often back down when confronted. Mean people and haters flourish on the Internet. Unplug and take a break from social media any time it is not serving you well. Doing so will feel strange at first, but it is a vacation, and that void can be medicine.

Not all friendships are forever. Some people are in your life for a season, and some will walk with you throughout your life. Friendships often fade. And friends might betray you. It's okay to save yourself and let a friend go for your own well-being. In some cases, you can keep the friend and redefine the relationship.

Some people will take advantage and suck the life out of you. Don't let others drain your energy. Your time and energy are assets. Guard them and use them wisely. Pick your friends by their values and character. Be choosy. True friends will champion you.

You will encounter self-serving people. Protect yourself. Avoid those who revel in drama. And when people show you who they really are, believe them. Do not make excuses for the bad behavior of others.

People have unique perspectives based on their upbringing or educational, cultural, and religious experiences. It's comforting to engage with like-minded people but listen to others who are different and seek to understand their perspectives. There will be times when you will not be able to do so. People can be weird or too far out there to enjoy. You decide who you let into your life. Tolerance has its limits.

In social settings, it is often best to match the energy level of others in a group. Avoid being the hyped-up person everyone stares at. On the other hand, if the energy of a group of people gets too ramped up, be the one who calms things down.

Sometimes love hurts. Don't despair. Love is the ultimate gift—a rare and precious one. Embrace it. Relish it. And treasure it—even when it fades. The first love is especially hard. The pain is new. You will most likely have many loves during your life and many hurts—each one a blessing because each one is the bearer of lessons that leave you wiser and stronger. Make your teenage children aware of the nuances of romantic love.

FAMILY

You Were Born into a Tribe, and That Is No Little Thing

Your family is a team. You owe an allegiance to its members. Respect your parents. Nurture and champion siblings. Defend family members. Be loyal to them. Avoid spreading negative information about them. However, recognize that every family has some level of dysfunction. In some circumstances, a line can be crossed, which requires self-care to take precedence over the well-being of others. In such instances, seek counseling, even if other family members do not.

Most parents do the best they can with what they know and what they have. You will be a parent someday, and you will not execute that role perfectly. Judge your parents gently. You may never know the demons with which they wrestled.

Your children's journey is different from yours. Don't consider them wrong because they are not like you. Their innate talents, temperaments, and personalities may be different from yours. They may naturally perceive the world differently. Respect that. In difficult times, when parenting overwhelms—and it will—remember: parenting is your job. Do it.

It is unreasonable to expect seniors in high school to know what profession they want to go into as adults. This will be discovered as they continue their education and experience life. Be careful about pressuring them for decisions.

WORK

Leadership Is Service to Others

Be responsible when you get a job. Go to work every day and on time no matter what. Don't call in sick because you are tired, have had a rough weekend, have allergies, or things are going to be tough at the worksite that day. When you miss work, you let work teammates and customers down. Transitioning from school with all its time off will require adjustment to a full-time job with more demanding schedules.

Show up. Tough days you dread often turn out not to be as terrible as you thought they would be. You'll be glad you bucked up and did the right thing.

Before teenagers secure their first jobs, educate them on controls employers have to identify employee theft. Never ever steal from an employer or allow friends to talk you into giving them free products. You will get caught.

If work becomes intolerable, try quitting your job in your mind but go to work every day. This is a coping strategy that allows you to mellow out, which fosters endurance by easing pressures. Ultimately, problems often melt away or fade in significance. Here is another instance when *this too-shall-pass* mentality can be helpful. When you pull back, reset priorities, and focus on work relationships and the basics of your job rather than the things that trouble you, work will most likely smooth out in many ways. Seek balance. You can do too much or too little of anything.

EMBRACE RATIONAL THOUGHT

Don't Be a Patsy. Think for Yourself

Some very smart people believe some crazy things. Don't do that. Critical thinking based on facts is vital to drawing valid conclusions and not appearing ignorant.

What you and other people think in your heads is a story. Stories are not facts. Thoughts are not facts. Opinions are not facts. Facts are facts. Thoughts can become beliefs, which are often based on a story rather than on factual information. For that reason, beliefs can lead to unfortunate conclusions, behaviors, and outcomes. When forming beliefs, base them on the reality of facts. When you observe a nut job, you will almost always see a person lacking in critical thinking.

Bullies and opportunists use labels to influence and take advantage. Labels are often used for political manipulation through insinuations not based on facts. Name-calling puts a label on a person or a political or societal concept. (Example: proposed legislation for healthcare labeled as a *scheme*.) Watch out for labels. Investigate facts before accepting one. Draw conclusions on facts, not labels assigned by others.

Avoid *groupthink*. Just because many other people believe something, does not make it true. Never underestimate the mailability of the human brain and the ability of someone to manipulate others through techniques that reshape brain chemistry. Be cognizant of motives, and the power of persuasion. Familiarize yourself with cult-building techniques. Think for yourself.

Learn to distinguish between news reporting, commentary, and propaganda. Years ago, news stations were objective in their reporting. This is no longer true. These days, much of what is presented as news is not fact-based. It is propaganda designed by greedy, power-mongering people who consider themselves entitled. They use stories rather than facts to convince people to act against their own best interests.

Propaganda machines try to limit your access to information to one source—theirs. This is so they can influence and take advantage. Don't fall for it. Seek information from multiple sources. Through their propaganda, they manipulate people to act against their own best interests. Be cognizant of sources of information and the people behind the so-called news.

Some people have a bucket list of things they dream of doing. Consider also having an *anti-bucket list* of things you don't want to do. And, of course, don't do them. One of those things is to blindly follow others.

When so many bad things happen that you think you can't take anymore, you can.

***

That's a lot of information, I know. Do with it what you will. Think for yourself and shape your life accordingly. Above all else, know you are valuable and have a life purpose. Seek to discover that purpose by tapping into your innate, unique talents so you are equipped to live a purposeful life and make the world a better place. Living that way will bring you joy. I promise. And most importantly, go easy on yourself. You deserve a crazy wonderful life just because you are here.

CITATIONS

Preface

All Poetry. Emily Dickinson. "If I Can Stop One Heart From Breaking."
Poem. Publisher. Little, Brown, and Company, Boston, MA. 1929.
https://allpoetry.com/if-i-can-stop-

YouTube. Capitol Records. Helen Reddy "I Am Woman" (Australian TV
Special / 1975 / HQ) Video, 4:15
https://www.youtube.com/watch?v=Fr1ObOl7DVw

Chapter 1

YouTube. Mercury Records. Donna Summer. "She Works Hard for the
Money." Video, 4:08.
https://www.youtube.com/watch?v=N8EkGUm9q_A

Wikipedia: "Radio City Music Hall Rockettes" Nov. 12, 2011
https://en.wikipedia.org/wiki/The_Rockettes

Chapter 2

Wikipedia. Warner Bros. "The Bridges of Madison County." Film, 134 minutes. Release Date, June 2, 1995. https://en.wikipedia.org/wiki/The_Bridges_of_Madison_County_(film)

Chapter 5

YouTube. Columbia Records. Artist - The Birds. "Turn, Turn, Turn." Video, 3:49. https://www.youtube.com/watch?v=xVOJla2vYx8

YouTube. □ 1973 UMG Recordings, Inc. Lynyrd Skynyrd. "Free Bird." Audio File. 9:18. https://www.youtube.com/watch?v=IGLVMBTIAPE

Chapter 7

Wikipedia. Beacon Press. Mary Oliver. "The Uses of Sorrow." Poem. https://en.wikipedia.org/wiki/Mary_Oliver#Poetry_collections

YouTube. Columbia Records. Artist - The Birds. "Turn, Turn, Turn." Video, 3:49. https://www.youtube.com/watch?v=xVOJla2vYx8

YouTube. Capitol Records. Helen Reddy. "I Am Woman." (Australian TV Special / 1973 / HQ Video, 4:15 https://www.youtube.com/watch?v=Fr1ObOl7DVw

Chapter 8

YouTube. RCA Victor. Elvis Presley. "All Shook Up." Audio, 1:58.
https://www.youtube.com/watch?v=23zLefwiii4

Chapter 9

YouTube. Capitol Records. Helen Reddy. "I Am Woman." (Australian TV
Special / 1973 / HQ Video, 4:15
https://www.youtube.com/watch?v=Fr1ObOl7DVw

Wikipedia. Universal Pictures. "Field of Dreams."
Film, 108 minutes. Release Date, May 5, 1989.
https://en.wikipedia.org/wiki/Field_of_Dreams

Wikipedia. Warner Bros. "The Bridges of Madison County." (film) Film,
134 minutes. Release Date, June 2, 1995.
https://en.wikipedia.org/wiki/The_Bridges_of_Madison_County_(film
)

Chapter 11

Theodore Roosevelt Center. Theodore Roosevelt. "The Man in the Arena."
Speech. April 23, 1910.
https://www.theodorerooseveltcenter.org/Learn-About-TR/TR-Encycl
opedia/Culture-and-Society/Man-in-the-Arena.aspx

Chapter 15

YouTube. Warner Bros. Records. John Fogerty. "Centerfield." Video.
3:51.
https://www.youtube.com/watch?v=Xq3hEMUeBGQ

Chapter 18

Poetry Society of America. Harper Collins. Copyright © 1995 by Coleman Barks. Rumi. "Out Beyond Ideas of Wrongdoing and Rightdoing." Poem.
https://poetrysociety.org/poetry-in-motion/out-beyond-ideas-of-wrongdoing-and-rightdoing

Chapter 20

Bible Gateway. Matthew 6:9-13. "The Lord's Prayer." Bible Verses.
https://www.biblegateway.com/passage/?search=Matthew%206%3A9-13&version=KJV#:~:text=%E2%80%94Amuzgo%20de%20Guerrero%20(AMU),Matthew%207

Chapter 21

Wikipedia. June Carter Cash. "Singer and Songwriter."
https://en.wikipedia.org/wiki/June_Carter_Cash

Wikipedia. George Bernard Shaw. "Irish playwright, critic, polemicist, and political activist."
https://en.wikipedia.org/wiki/George_Bernard_Shaw

Wikipedia. 14th Dalai Lama. Easton Press. "The Art of Happiness." Book.
https://en.wikipedia.org/wiki/The_Art_of_Happiness

All Poetry. Ralph Waldo Emerson. "To Laugh Often and Much." Publisher. James Munroe. 1905.

https://allpoetry.com/poem/14327880-To-Laugh-Often-And-Much-by-Ralph-Waldo-Emerson

Avidly. Bessie A. Stanley. "To Laugh Often and Much." Emporia (Kansas) Gazette 1906 https://avidly.lareviewofbooks.org/2019/08/27/on-fake-emerson-quotes/

Epilogue

Wikipedia. Oprah Winfrey. "American talk show host, television producer, actress, author, and media proprietor." https://en.wikipedia.org/wiki/Oprah_Winfrey

ABOUT THE AUTHOR

Through a compelling and entertaining memoir, Joan Sandergard's resounding story of hope and resilience inspires readers to rally from unfortunate experiences to become a person of purpose. After her struggles to endure and overcome traumatic incidents during her pre-teen and early adult years, she evolved into a woman dedicated to improving the lives of others. This introduced a stunning rally. Rich with wisdom and lessons learned her story shows how to overcome anything. Bold and candid, she bravely examines her complicated and, at times, torturous past. Her life review reveals how self-awareness and endurance can triumph over adversity.

She served as a Child Advocate for D.V.I.S. and worked with other youth services developing programs for teen substance abuse. She worked for twenty-three years in multiple roles in the Oklahoma State Welfare Agency where she dedicated her life to advocating for children and families. During her last five years at the Agency, she served as District Director for Child Welfare Services. There her leadership and administrative abilities influenced programs affecting the lives of disadvantaged families and enhanced the state of the community.

She served as a member of the District Attorney's Task Force, Child Protection Coalition, Oklahoma State Tribal Group, Child Trafficking

Task Force, and board member for Tulsa Advocates for Protection of Children (TAPC). Other positions of service included board member of the First Wings of Freedom Area Advisory Council, member of the Tobacco-free coalition, and other community task forces. A frequent presenter in the community, she was a champion for children and families.

Sandergard has a B.S. degree in Education from Drake University and thirty graduate hours in a Master of Divinity program as well as a Substance Abuse Counselor Certification and Teachers Certification in the state of Oklahoma.

The Lessons Learned section featured in this memoir is lush with practical wisdom. It introduces perspectives that have the potential to change lives. This thoughtful information is designed to benefit anyone of any age, based on her willingness to reveal the valleys of her past so these lessons can be shared.

Sandergard leaves the reader with strong messages on how to overcome and live a purposeful life—to believe, rise up, and never give up hope. She writes with joy and purpose.